Getting Skills Right

Career Guidance for Adults in Canada

OECD
BETTER POLICIES FOR BETTER LIVES

This work is published under the responsibility of the Secretary-General of the OECD. The opinions expressed and arguments employed herein do not necessarily reflect the official views of the Member countries of the OECD.

This document, as well as any data and map included herein, are without prejudice to the status of or sovereignty over any territory, to the delimitation of international frontiers and boundaries and to the name of any territory, city or area.

Please cite this publication as:
OECD (2022), *Career Guidance for Adults in Canada*, Getting Skills Right, OECD Publishing, Paris, https://doi.org/10.1787/0e596882-en.

ISBN 978-92-64-44676-2 (print)
ISBN 978-92-64-69365-4 (pdf)

Getting Skills Right
ISSN 2520-6117 (print)
ISSN 2520-6125 (online)

Foreword

The world of work is changing. Digitalisation, globalisation, the green transition and population ageing are having a profound impact on the type and quality of jobs that are available and the skills required to perform them. The extent to which individuals, firms and economies can reap the benefits of these changes will depend critically on the readiness of adult learning systems to help people develop and maintain relevant skills over their working careers.

Career guidance for adults is a fundamental policy lever to motivate adults to train and to help address the challenges brought about by rapidly changing skill needs. Such services are particularly important amid the ongoing COVID-19 pandemic and its aftermath, as many adults have lost their job and require assistance in navigating their career options in the rapidly evolving labour market.

To explore this issue, the OECD has undertaken an ambitious programme of work on the functioning, effectiveness and resilience of adult career guidance systems across countries. As part of this project, the OECD carried out an online survey in 10 countries (Argentina, Brazil, Canada, Chile, Mexico, New Zealand, France, Germany, Italy, and the United States) between 2020 and 2021 to better understand the user experience of adults with career guidance, and any barriers adults might face in accessing these services. The OECD also prepared a policy questionnaire to collect information on good practices across OECD countries in the area of career guidance for adults.

This report provides a review of career guidance in Canada. Chapter 1 presents the current Canadian labour market context and provides an overview of the system of career guidance across the Canadian provinces and territories. Chapter 2 assesses the coverage and inclusiveness of career guidance services, with a particular focus on vulnerable adults. Chapter 3 reviews different dimensions of quality in career guidance and suggests policy measures to improve service provision. In addition to new survey evidence, the analysis of the report draws on interviews with Canadian stakeholders and policy questionnaires completed by federal and provincial ministries.

Magdalena Burtscher and Katharine Mullock from the Skills and Employability Division of the Directorate for Employment, Labour and Social Affairs are the authors of this report. Erika Xiomara Chaparro Pérez provided valuable statistical research. The work was carried out under the supervision of Glenda Quintini (Manager of the Skills Team) and Mark Keese (Head of the Skills and Employability Division) and benefited from helpful contributions from members of the Skills team. Special thanks are due to the many Canadian stakeholders for sharing their expertise and insights during virtual interviews in June and July 2021, and to the Future Skills Centre and Labour Market Information Council for their active collaboration.

This report is published under the responsibility of the Secretary-General of the OECD, with the financial assistance of the Future Skills Centre and the Labour Market Information Council. The views expressed in this report should not be taken to reflect the official position of the Government of Canada nor those of any other OECD member country.

Table of contents

FIGURES

TABLES

Follow OECD Publications on:

>>

http://twitter.com/OECD_Pubs

http://www.facebook.com/OECDPublications

http://www.linkedin.com/groups/OECD-Publications-4645871

http://www.youtube.com/oecdilibrary

http://www.oecd.org/oecddirect/

Acronyms and abbreviations

AI	Artificial intelligence
CCDF	Canadian Career Development Foundation
CDP	Career Development Practitioner
CCDP	Certified Career Development Practitioner
CDI	Career Development Institute, United Kingdom
CEIS	Career and Employment Information Services, Alberta
CERIC	Canadian Education and Research Institute for Counselling
CLARS	Coordinated Language Assessment and Referral System, Ontario
CPMT	Commission des Partenaires du Marchés du Travail, Quebec
CEP	Conseil en Évolution Professionnelle, France
C.O.	Conseillers et Conseillères d'Orientation (Guidance Counsellors), Quebec
CPC	Career Professionals Canada
ECGC	European Career Guidance Certificate
ESDC	Employment and Social Development Canada
ESPP	Employment Success Package Programme, Korea
FLMM	Forum of Labour Market Ministers
FSC	Future Skills Centre
GDP	Gross domestic product
GOAL	Guidance and Orientation for Adult Learners, EU project
IAEVG	International Association for Educational and Vocational Guidance
ICT	Information and communications technology
KPI	Key performance indicator
LMDA	Labour Market Development Agreement
LMI	Labour Market Information
LMIC	Labour Market Information Council
NCI	National Career Institute, Australia
NCGE	National Centre for Guidance in Education, Ireland
NGO	Non-governmental organisation
OCCOQ	Ordre des conseillers et conseillères d'orientation du Québec
OECD	Organisation for Economic Co-operation and Development
PAL	Priorities for Adult Learning Dashboard
PARAF	Programme pour la requalification et l'augmentation de la formation (Renewed Prosperity Through Greater Training Program), Quebec
PCM	People and Communities in Motion, Quebec
PES	Public employment service
PIAAC	Programme for the International Assessment of Adult Competencies (OECD Survey of Adult Skills)
PLAR	Prior learning assessment and recognition
PRACTIC	Programme pour la requalification et l'accompagnement en technologies de l'informations et communications (Information and communication technology requalification and training program), Quebec
PRIME	Performance Recording Instrument for Meaningful Evaluation
RAC	Reconnaissance des acquis et des compétences (recognition of prior learning), Quebec
SARCA	Services d'accueil, de référence, de conseil et d'accompagnement (Reception, referral, counselling and support services), Quebec
SCGA	OECD Survey of Career Guidance for Adults
S&Gs	Canadian Standards and Guidelines for Career Development Practitioners
SMEs	Small and medium-sized enterprises
VET	Vocational education and training
WDA	Workforce Development Agreement

Canadian Provinces and Territories	
AB	Alberta
BC	British Columbia
MB	Manitoba
NB	New Brunswick
NL	Newfoundland and Labrador
NS	Nova Scotia
NT	Northwest Territories
NU	Nunavut
ON	Ontario
PE	Prince Edward Island
QC	Quebec
SK	Saskatchewan
YT	Yukon

Executive summary

The COVID-19 pandemic has had a profound impact on the Canadian labour market, deepening existing divides and changing the demand for skills. Already prior to the pandemic, labour demand was changing due to the adoption of new digital technology, population ageing, globalisation and decarbonisation. The skills needs for jobs in growing sectors and industries are often not the same as those required for jobs that are at risk of automation or outsourcing. In this context, many adults are being challenged to consider alternative career paths, and to upskill or retrain.

A growing body of international evidence suggests that career guidance has the potential to support successful employment transitions: not only from the education system to the labour market, but also from unemployment to employment, and from declining to growing sectors. In this way, it can support the post-pandemic recovery by facilitating career transitions and bolstering the labour market participation of vulnerable groups.

This study takes stock of career guidance services for adults in Canada, and puts them into international perspective. It relies on new international survey evidence from the OECD Survey of Career Guidance for Adults (SCGA), interviews with key Canadian stakeholders, and policy questionnaires completed by federal and provincial ministries.

Adults in Canada use career guidance services less than adults in a number of other OECD countries. According to the SCGA, only 19% of Canadian adults used a career service over the past five years. This is nearly half of the average across countries in the survey (39%). The lower use of career services in Canada reflects that Canadian adults are less likely than their international counterparts to seek guidance when choosing a study or training programme (19% versus 31%), or when they want to progress in their current job (27% versus 40%). Employed adults in Canada are also less likely to use career services than the unemployed, which is not the case in other countries. The most common reason that adults stated for not using career services was not feeling the need to, and this is in common with other countries in the survey. Unlike in other countries, however, adults in Canada were more likely to report that they did not have enough time due to either work or family/childcare responsibilities.

Low-educated adults, older adults and those living in rural areas in Canada are less likely to use career guidance services than other groups, common to what is also observed in other OECD countries. This is a source of concern, since these groups often experience intersecting barriers to employment and face a higher risk of skills obsolescence and job automation than other groups more involved in career guidance. In Canada, inclusion in service provision is a particularly pressing issue: contrary to those in other OECD countries, adults in Canada who feel negative about their future labour market prospects are actually less likely to seek career guidance than those who feel more positive. More active outreach and a better targeting of services is essential to support greater use of career guidance by vulnerable groups. In Australia, for instance, Victoria's public employment services sends "advocates" out into the community to connect with vulnerable adults wherever they are, including in libraries, community centres, public housing foyers, shopping centres and other places offering community services. At the same time, the European pilot project GOAL demonstrates how active outreach and addressing the complex needs of vulnerable groups through career guidance can be effective in raising their participation in adult learning, even if it requires considerable investment.

The most common providers of adult career services in Canada are government-run employment services and private career guidance providers. Government-run employment services delivered by the provinces have a job matching focus, and tend to target unemployed adults. Employed adults are more likely to consult career services offered by private providers, though these come at a cost. Adults who face a high risk of job automation tend to be older and lower-skilled and may not be able to afford these private services. In the current context of rapidly changing demand for skills and the need to reach out to workers ahead of job loss, this is a significant gap in service provision. Experiences from Germany and Flanders (Belgium) show how government-funded employment services can take a more proactive approach by building their capacity to serve both unemployed and employed workers.

In Canada, the responsibility for adult career guidance policy is shared between different levels of government and stakeholder bodies. Policy-making on adult career guidance is shaped by federal-provincial funding agreements relating to employment services, cross-ministerial co-operation through working groups, and the work of different stakeholder bodies to support policy co-ordination. However, there is no strategic development of career guidance policy on a federal or provincial level. Some OECD countries, such as Australia, Ireland, and Norway have dedicated public bodies to co-ordinate career guidance across ministries and levels of government.

Canada performs well compared to OECD countries with respect to the quality of career guidance, though there is room to improve consistency in service provision. Adults' satisfaction with career services in Canada is on par with other countries, and adults in Canada were more likely to indicate that career guidance services were useful to achieving reported employment and training outcomes. The report explores a number of ways Canada could make quality improvements in order to maintain this strong performance. Provinces could be more systematic about monitoring outcomes in line with long-term policy objectives. Nova Scotia Work's performance-related funding and Saskatchewan's use of the PRIME Employability Assessment Tool are innovative examples in this regard. Career guidance advisors could also be better supported in navigating and drawing meaningful insights from complex labour market information, possibly through regular training sessions about labour market developments as is done in France and Belgium. Finally, Canada is an OECD leader in the development of a competency framework for Career Development Professionals, which is the basis for the pan-Canadian certification for career guidance advisors currently under development. Supporting the implementation of this voluntary, pan-Canadian certification could help to establish a common standard of practice that might also improve consistency in service delivery within and across provinces and territories.

The box below summarises nine recommendations to strengthen co-ordination of adult career guidance policy in Canada, to encourage greater and more inclusive use of adult career services, and to promote high-quality service provision.

Key recommendations

Strengthen co-ordination of career guidance policy and provision

- Federal, provincial and territorial governments should co-ordinate, possibly through the Forum of Labour Market Ministers or another body designated with this co-ordination role, to develop a strategy for adult career guidance in Canada.

- Strengthen the capacity of the provincial government-run employment services to create proactive career guidance opportunities for adults in employment at risk of job loss or with poor career prospects.

- Improve co-operation between training providers, government-run employment services and employers with the objective of supporting the provision of neutral career and training guidance for adults.

- Government-run employment services should continue to offer a mix of face-to-face and remote guidance services, but expand face-to-face provision to meet client demand when sanitary conditions permit.

Fostering a greater and more inclusive use of career guidance services

- To raise awareness about career guidance services, provinces and territories should strengthen referrals between public services and launch a media campaign.

- Provincial and territorial governments should dedicate funding to actively reach out to vulnerable adults in their communities and workplaces and better target career guidance services to their needs.

Promote high-quality career guidance service provision

- Provinces and territories should systematically monitor the outcomes of publicly-funded career guidance services in line with long-term policy objectives.

- Provinces and territories should strengthen training for advisors providing career guidance in publicly-funded services, especially on the use of labour market information.

- Federal, provincial and territorial governments should in co-ordination support and fund the implementation of a voluntary, pan-Canadian certification for career development practitioners.

1 Career guidance to support the recovery in Canada

Canadian labour markets have been severely affected by the COVID-19 pandemic, which has highlighted the importance of a skilled and resilient workforce that is able to navigate employment transitions. This chapter first provides an overview of the impact of the pandemic, as well as the longer-term trends of technological change, globalisation, population ageing and decarbonisation, on Canadian labour markets. It then reviews Canada's current performance in skilling adults. Finally, the chapter provides an outline of Canada's system of career guidance for adults, including how responsibility is shared, who the main providers are and how services are delivered.

Summary

The impact of the COVID-19 pandemic on output and employment was unprecedented, leading to record numbers of unemployed. But not all sectors and workers were affected in the same way. Industries that were able to switch to remote working and digital service provision were less impacted. The employment impact was greatest on young people, low-skilled and low-wage workers, women as well as minority groups, including Indigenous people. These groups have benefited from the employment recovery, but remain more vulnerable to reductions in working hours or employment losses resulting from new waves of infections.

Already prior to the pandemic, the demand for skills was changing due to technological adoption, population ageing, globalisation and decarbonisation. The pandemic has amplified ongoing trends that are putting certain groups of workers at risk of skills obsolescence and job automation. Adult learning, accompanied by career guidance, is a key policy lever to support the post-pandemic employment recovery. According to a growing body of international evidence, career guidance, which comprises a range of services that assist individuals to make well-informed choices about work and learning, has the potential to facilitate successful labour market transitions and to help counteract a long-term deepening of the divide between socio-economic groups.

Responsibility for adult career guidance, or career development as it is often called in Canada, is shared between different levels and areas of government. However, there is little strategic development of career guidance policy in Canada. The most common providers of career guidance to adults in Canada are provincially/territorially government-run employment services and private career guidance services. While the former are mostly targeted to unemployed workers, the latter can be costly for individuals, posing a challenge to a proactive, inclusive and lifelong approach to career guidance in Canada.

This chapter presents the current labour market context in Canada and provides an overview of the system of career guidance policy and provision for adults across provinces and territories. It highlights how structural changes in the demand for skills as a result of globalisation, technological change, population ageing and decarbonisation have been amplified by the COVID-19 crisis. In this context, adult skill development is more important than ever. There is growing evidence internationally that career guidance can motivate adults, and particularly those who are most vulnerable in the labour market, to access adult learning opportunities that will support their employability and their ability to adapt to labour market change (see Box 3.1).

In the context of this study, the term "career guidance" is used to refer to a range of services intended to assist individuals of all age groups to make well-informed educational, training and occupational choices and to manage their careers (see Box 1.1). While career guidance has traditionally focused on young people, this report focuses on services for adults who have already entered the labour market. To facilitate measurement, the focus is restricted to adults aged 25-64, while recognising that many adults stay in the labour market much later than age 64, and can continue to benefit from career guidance and learning opportunities well beyond age 64.

The analysis in this report draws from three sources: virtual interviews with Canadian stakeholders, a policy questionnaire that was completed by federal and provincial ministries of employment and provincial and territorial ministries of education, and the OECD Survey of Career Guidance for Adults (SCGA). The SCGA is an online survey that sheds light on the use, provision, inclusiveness, and quality of adult career guidance services across countries. In doing so, it fills an important information gap by creating an internationally-comparable source of data on the use of adult career guidance services. It was adapted to the Canadian context and implemented in Canada in June 2021, and, at the time of writing, had been carried out in nine other countries (Argentina, Brazil, Chile, Mexico, New Zealand, France, Germany, Italy, and the United States). The Annex provides more details about the policy questionnaire and the SCGA methodology.

1.1. A changing labour market context

The severe impact of the COVID-19 pandemic on employment coincided with ongoing transformations in Canadian labour markets. This section discusses how the impact of the pandemic on the Canadian labour markets as well as other ongoing structural changes such as digitalisation, demographic change and decarbonisation, have been transforming the demand for skills.

1.1.1. The COVID-19 crisis caused an unprecedented economic and employment shock

The COVID-19 pandemic led to an unprecedented economic and employment crisis in Canada and around the world. The measures to contain and mitigate the spread of the virus, combined with great uncertainty about the global outlook resulted in an immediate drop of economic activity. Similar to other OECD countries, real GDP dropped by 15% in Canada during the first wave of the pandemic, far exceeding the impact of the 2008/2009 global financial crisis. Economic output rebounded rapidly in the second half of 2020 and continued somewhat unevenly during 2021 (OECD, 2021[1]).

Prior to the pandemic, the country had experienced a steady employment growth since 2009, with record-low unemployment of 5.7% in 2019 and tight labour market conditions. As a result of sanitary containment measures, in seasonally adjusted terms, the unemployment rate peaked at nearly 13.5%, and total employment losses from February to April 2020 amounted to 3 million. The initial lockdowns led to a sharp rise in long-term unemployment,[1] visible in the third quarter of 2020 (Statistics Canada, 2021[2]). By November 2021, the unemployment rate had fallen to 6.1%, compared with 5.5% on average in the OECD, and just above its pre-pandemic levels (OECD, 2021[3]). Long-term unemployment is falling, but at 24% remains above the pre-crisis level of 16% in February 2020 (Statistics Canada, 2022[4]). Some softening of the labour market occurred in January 2022 as a result of the return of stricter public health measures in response to the surge in COVID-19 infections linked to the Omicron variant.

Figure 1.1. Employment and unemployment during the pandemic

Quarterly employment and unemployment rates, age 15-64, 2017-21

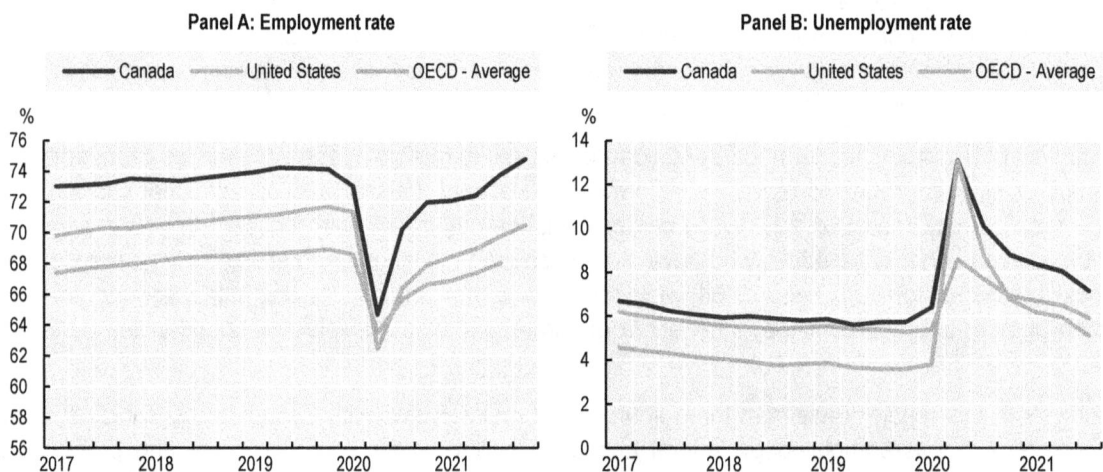

Note: The employment rate is defined as the employed population as a percentage of the working age population. The unemployment rate is defined as the unemployed population as a percentage of the labour force (active population). Labour force surveys in Canada and the United States classify temporary layoffs as being unemployed, in contrast to other OECD countries. As a result, those two countries saw sharper initial spikes in the rate of unemployment in the wake of the COVID-19 crisis.
Source: OECD (2021[5]), "Labour market statistics", *Main Economic Indicators* (database), https://doi.org/10.1787/data-00046-en (accessed on 22 June 2021).

The initial impact of the COVID-19 fell more heavily on some sectors and regions than others in response to social distancing measures, the temporary drop in consumer demand for some goods and services, and disruptions in global markets and supply chains. Services that rely on face-to-face interactions, non-essential spending and international movement experienced a more direct impact of containment and mitigation measures. Indeed, the accommodation and food service sector as well as arts, entertainment and recreation recorded the greatest declines in output and employment. Statistics Canada data show that these industries continued to experience lower monthly output in October 2021 compared to pre-pandemic levels (Statistics Canada, 2022[6]). Essential services, and those sectors which were able to adapt to the circumstances by shifting to telework or virtual service provision, saw a more moderate disruption of economic activity (Bank of Canada, 2021[7]). The effects of COVID-19 also differed across regions and provinces, as a result of variation in health care capacity, containment measures, and reliance on industries and sectors that were deeply hit (Bank of Canada, 2021[7]).

The federal and provincial governments in Canada adopted a range of programmes in order to help workers and firms through the crisis, to avoid layoffs and support the rehiring of employees. Examples of federal-level measures include: the Canada Emergency Wage Subsidy (CEWS), a temporary 75% wage subsidy for up to 24 weeks; easier access to credit for firms through a Business Credit Availability Program (BCAP); and the Canada Emergency Response Benefit (CERB) to support workers not covered or eligible for Employment Insurance (OECD, 2020[8]). These measures are likely to have contributed to the strong employment recovery since the trough of the crisis in April 2020.

At the end of 2021, with unemployment almost back to pre-pandemic levels, the employment recovery led to a substantial tightening in certain sectors. As the labour market conditions increasingly resemble those observed prior to the pandemic, they are likely to contribute to skills shortages across provincial, regional and local labour markets, as well as geographical mismatches between new job vacancies and the available workforce with relevant skills to fill them (Statistics Canada, 2021[9]).

1.1.2. Certain groups were hardest hit by the pandemic, deepening existing divides in labour markets

The employment contraction that followed the outbreak of the pandemic unevenly affected social and economic groups in Canada, deepening existing divides on Canadian labour markets. The greatest impacts were on young people, low-skilled workers, temporary employees and minority groups. Particularly hard-hit were young people under the age of 24, who accounted for 45% of the employment losses during 2020 (Statistics Canada, 2021[2]). Moreover, minorities, including Indigenous people, experienced a greater economic impact from the crisis, and higher levels of unemployment, financial difficulties, and representation in low-wage jobs (Statistics Canada, 2021[2]).

Labour force data from 2020 shows that women were more affected by initial employment losses than men, mainly due to their overrepresentation in the services sector. Women also saw a larger decrease in their paid hours than men, which might also be linked to them taking on additional care responsibilities during the closures of schools and childcare facilities. The recovery of female employment initially lagged behind that of male employment (LMIC-CIMT, 2021[10]), but caught up towards the end of 2021.

In contrast to the global financial crisis of 2009, new layoffs in 2020 disproportionally affected individuals at the lower end of the wage distribution (Figure 1.2). Low-wage workers have also experienced a larger drop in working hours than their higher-earning counterparts during the COVID-19 crisis. Wages and educational attainment are strongly linked (OECD, 2020[11]), and data suggests that low-skilled groups were overrepresented among those who became unemployed during the crisis.

Figure 1.2. Layoffs by wage group during COVID-19 and the financial crisis, Canada

Average monthly layoff rates of employees, by wage decile, 2009 and 2020

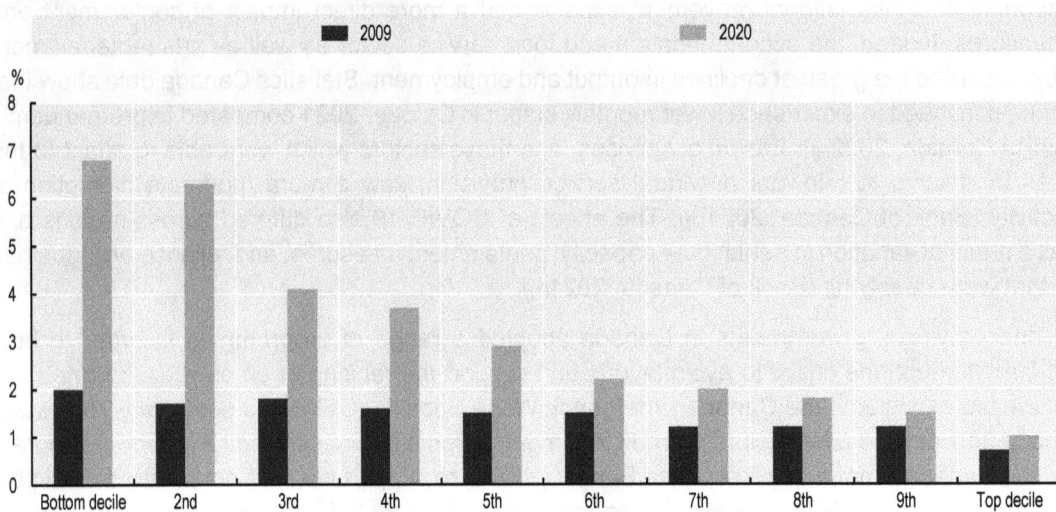

Note: Average month-to-month change from January 2020 to December 2020, all pairs of months for 2009.
Source: Statistics Canada (2021[2]), COVID-19 *in Canada: A One-year Update on Social and Economic Impacts*, https://www150.statcan.gc.ca/n1/pub/11-631-x/11-631-x2021001-eng.htm#a4 (accessed 10 October 2021).

While employment has nearly recovered to pre-pandemic levels on aggregate, the employment of some vulnerable groups may take longer to recover (OECD, 2021[12]). Vulnerable groups often face numerous and intersecting employment obstacles, such as limited work experience, care obligations, low skills or health limitations. Previous crises have shown that economic downturns can have longer-term scarring effects on the employment outcomes of young people who enter the labour market during the time of crisis (Andrews et al., 2020[13]; Bell and Blanchflower, 2011[14]). It remains to be seen, at the time of writing, whether government measures such as additional funding for the Youth Employment and Skills Strategy will help to prevent such negative effects.

OECD analysis has shown an association between workers' vulnerability to technological change and the intensity with which the crisis hit them (OECD, 2021[12]). In particular, workers whose skills and occupations were in low demand and at higher risk of automation prior to the pandemic were more likely to lose their jobs in 2020, while their higher-skilled peers were more likely to experience a reduction in working time, and a shift to remote working (OECD, 2021[12]). Workers in jobs at a higher risk of automation might have experienced a weaker employment recovery and might be challenged to change their occupation, given the accelerated reorganisation of work and adoption of new technologies in the labour market since the onset of the crisis (OECD, 2021[12]; McKinsey Global Institute, 2021[15]).

1.1.3. The demand for skills was disrupted by COVID-19, but was already undergoing major changes before

While overall the number of vacancies and new hires dropped during the pandemic, online vacancy data suggest that certain occupations and skills continued to be in high demand in Canada (OECD, 2021[16]). Health care professionals such as physicians, nurses, pharmacists, epidemiologists, care assistants or technicians saw a particularly strong increase in demand in 2020. Among the skills most required during the pandemic were technical skills related to health and transversal skills, including communication, teamwork and customer service skills (OECD, 2021[16]). Future-proof jobs in Canada will likely continue to require high levels of cognitive skills, digital skills as well as social and emotional skills, including management, communication, leadership and self-organisation skills (OECD, 2020[17]; 2019[18]).

At the same time, labour markets were undergoing transformations even before COVID-19 due to technological change, globalisation, population ageing and the shift to a low-carbon economy. Preliminary evidence suggests that the pandemic has accelerated ongoing automation and the adoption of digital technologies, as many companies switched to remote working, started offering digital services, or transitioned to more digital business processes. While this change provided opportunities for many, workers in low-skilled occupations often were not able to telework, and are likely to face a higher risk of having obsolete skills due to digitalisation and automation (Nedelkoska and Quintini, 2018[19]).

Figure 1.3. Jobs at risk of automation or significant change

Share of jobs at high risk of automation or significant change, percentage

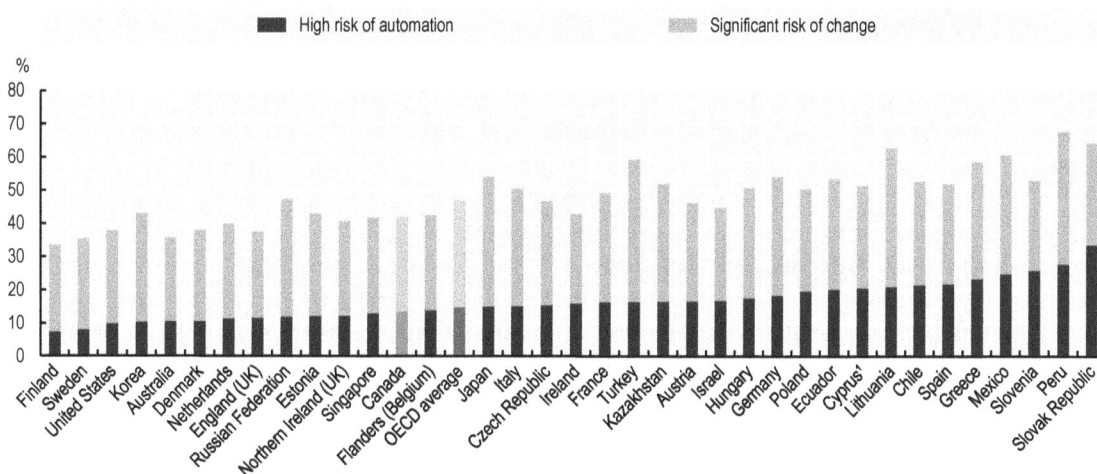

Note: Jobs are at high risk of automation if the likelihood of their job being automated is at least 70%. Jobs at risk of significant change are those with the likelihood of their job being automated estimated at between 50 and 70%.
Source: OECD calculations based on the Survey of Adult Skills (PIAAC, 2012); and Nedelkoska and Quintini (2018[19]) "Automation, skills use and training", *OECD Social, Employment and Migration Working Papers*, No. 202, https://doi.org/10.1787/2e2f4eea-en.

According to OECD estimates based on data for 2012, 13% of jobs in Canada were at high risk of automation while an additional 30% approximately were at significant risk of change due to automation because many tasks, but not all, could be automated (Figure 1.3). The Advisory Council on Economic Growth estimates that almost a quarter of all tasks performed by Canadian workers could be displaced by technology by 2030 (2017[20]). Given the acceleration of trends in remote work, digital business practices and automation during the pandemic, this number might have increased. In a 2021 publication, the McKinsey Global Institute predicts that 25% more workers than previously estimated will need to switch occupations (McKinsey Global Institute, 2021[15]). While job losses due to technological change might well be offset by new jobs, emerging industries will require different skills and qualifications than those that are in decline. In particular, digital skills will likely be required in more jobs, and not only in those relating to information technology. From this perspective, upskilling and reskilling opportunities, as well as career guidance for workers to reorient themselves, are essential.

The ageing of the population is another long-term trend that puts pressure on Canadian labour markets and changes the demand for skills. The number of individuals aged 65 and over per 100 people of working age (20-64), is projected to almost double, from 26 in 2015 to 48 by 2050 (OECD, 2017[21]). On the one hand, this will result in a shrinking workforce, while creating more demand for health and care services, which is likely to put pressure on public budgets. On the other hand, older people might be able to remain in the workforce longer due to increases in life expectancy, emphasising the need for lifelong learning and access to skills training.

Finally, the transition to a low-carbon economy as a response to climate change and environmental pressures is likely to affect Canadian labour markets by displacing employment in the traditional energy sector and related fields. Canada has committed to reducing greenhouse gas emissions by 30% below 2005 levels by 2030 under the Paris Agreement, and has announced a target to achieve net-zero emissions by 2050, together with 72 other countries. Reaching this goal requires reducing emissions in the energy sector, which accounted for 832 000 direct and indirect jobs in 2018, or 4.4% of total employment in Canada (Government of Canada, 2021[22]). While the government foresees the clean energy transition creating up to 350 000 new jobs in the hydrogen sector across Canada (Government of Canada, 2020[23]), up to 50-75% of workers currently employed in the oil and gas sector could be displaced, according to one estimate (Caranci, Fong and El Baba, 2021[24]). This represents 312 000 to 450 000 lost jobs, two-thirds of which are located in Alberta, Saskatchewan and Newfoundland and Labrador. Effective climate change mitigation will require a focus on jobs and skills, in particular to find ways that address geographically concentrated job displacement. While there might be no direct pathways for many people from declining industries to new employment opportunities in the clean energy sector, concerted efforts are required to facilitate the clean transition through skills, employment and community development strategies.

1.2. Skills and adult learning in Canada

While Canada has a highly educated population, it is not among the best performers in terms of the skills of adults. It has the highest share of adults with tertiary education (58% compared to the OECD average of 37%). However, the OECD Survey of Adult Skills (PIAAC) places the skills of Canadian adults above the OECD average, but below adults in the best-performing countries. An important share of the Canadian population (27%) has low proficiency in either literacy or numeracy, scoring at level 0 or 1 (OECD, 2019[25]).

A part of the discrepancy between educational attainment and the skills proficiency of adults might be linked to weaknesses in Canada's adult learning system, and the skills development of adults over their lifetime. The Advisory Council on Economic Growth argued that while Canada has good systems to support initial educational attainment and to help those who are unemployed or retired, it lags behind in the institutional framework and assistance available for the skills development of the working-age population (Advisory Council on Economic Growth, 2017[20]).

The following section briefly reviews Canada's performance on adult learning based on international comparisons.

1.2.1. Many adults in Canada continue to learn or train, but the system could be more inclusive

According to the OECD Priorities for Adult Learning dashboard,[2] Canada performs significantly above the OECD average in terms of the coverage and financing of adult learning, and the alignment of training with labour market needs. However, it performs comparatively poorly on inclusiveness (see Figure 1.4). In other dimensions measured by the dashboard (flexibility and guidance, financing, and perceived impact), Canada performs closer to the OECD average.

According to the data for 2012 from the OECD Survey of Adult Skills (PIAAC), 52% of Canadian adults aged 16 to 65 participated in some form of adult learning, be it formal, non-formal, or both, over the course of one year. On average, this places Canada well above the OECD average (41%), albeit below top-performing countries, including Denmark (59%), New Zealand (58%), or Finland (57%) (OECD, 2019[25]). There are also regional differences with participation rates slightly below the OECD average in Newfoundland and Labrador, as well as Nunavut (Government of Canada and Council of Ministers of Education, Canada, 2021[26]).

COVID-19 disrupted opportunities for upskilling and reskilling, and has likely affected the participation in adult learning temporarily. An international survey finds that training in firms and organisations was suspended for 86% of employees, 79% of apprentices, and 71% of interns or trainees in OECD countries. Workers in small and medium-sized enterprises were especially affected (ILO, 2021[27]). Despite a swift policy response that included a federal-level wage subsidy for employers to retain apprentices, new registrations and certifications in skilled trades decreased in the first three-quarters of 2020 by 43% and 49% respectively, compared to the same period in 2019 (Statistics Canada, 2021[2]).

Already prior to the pandemic, adults experienced barriers to participate in adult education and training. For almost one-third of Canadians who wanted to train but were unable to do so (30%), the main barrier cited was being too busy at work (OECD, 2020[17]). Women reported being too busy at work less often, but were twice as likely as men to cite family responsibilities as an impediment. Women were also less likely to receive employer support than men, although this could partially be due to differences in the type of jobs by gender (Government of Canada and Council of Ministers of Education, Canada, 2021[26]). Other barriers were the costs of training (19%), unsuitable time and place of training (17%), or not having the right prerequisites (2%) (OECD, 2020[17]).

As in other countries, participation in job-related adult learning in Canada correlates with factors such as age, skill level, wage, gender, minority or immigration background, and labour market status. Younger, higher-skilled and higher-earning individuals are more likely to participate in adult learning compared to their older, lower-skilled or low-income counterparts (see Figure 1.4). Gaps in participation also exist between Canadian-born adults and immigrants, women and men, as well as the Indigenous and non-Indigenous population, albeit to a smaller extent. Moreover, unemployed workers, those with temporary contracts or workers in small and medium-sized enterprises are less likely to participate in training than those who are employed, working in larger firms, or who have permanent contracts. The uneven participation in adult learning by different demographic groups means that educational and other inequalities are aggravated over the life course.

Figure 1.4. Participation gap in adult learning across demographic groups

Percentage point differences in training participation rates between groups, Canada and OECD

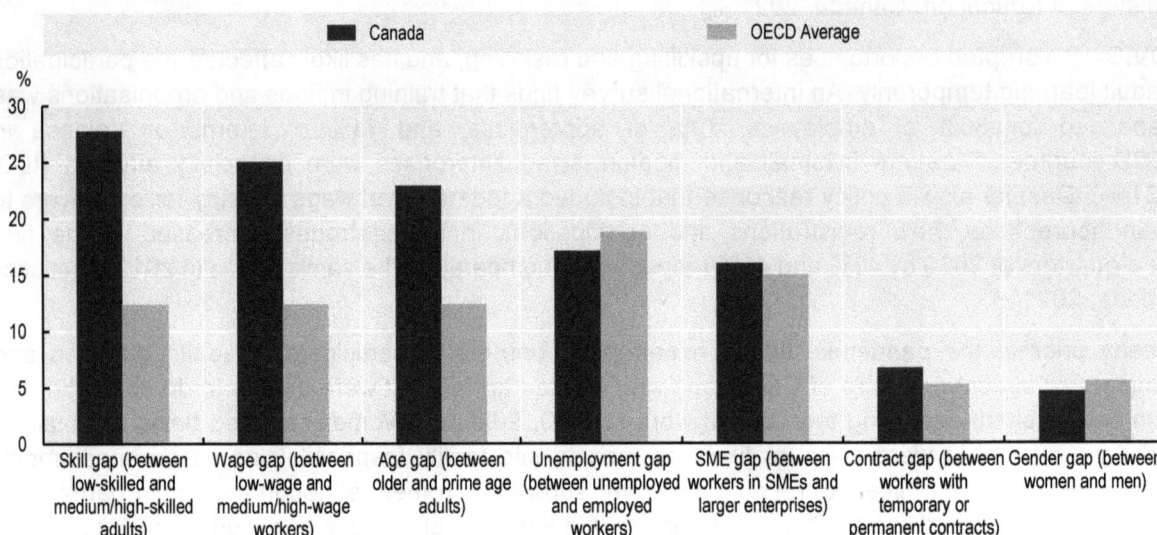

Note: Includes job-related formal and non-formal learning. The baseline varies across categories, e.g. low-skilled refers to all adults scoring at Level 1 or below in literacy and/or numeracy in PIAAC, low-wage refers to workers who earn at most two-thirds of the national median wage, temporary refers to workers in temporary contracts; workers in SMEs refers to workers in enterprises between 1 and 249 employees.
Source: OECD (2019[25]), *The Survey of Adult Skills: Reader's Companion, Third Edition*, https://dx.doi.org/10.1787/f70238c7-en.

Equipping adults with information and guidance about employment and training opportunities is an important part of adult learning systems. Career guidance can support adults in identifying reskilling and upskilling opportunities, and successfully manage employment transitions, which is especially important amid the economic recovery from COVID-19, and in the larger context of rapidly changing labour markets. A sharper focus on career guidance for adults in Canada could also support a more inclusive adult learning system by addressing inequalities in awareness of and knowledge about relevant training opportunities.

1.3. Career guidance for adults in Canada

Career guidance (or career development, as it is commonly known in Canada) assists individuals of all ages in making well-informed educational, training and occupational choices and in managing their careers (Box 1.4). For young people, it supports their decisions around higher education and training as well as their transitions into the labour market. Adults benefit from career guidance when they want to reskill or upskill, move to a new occupation or sector in the labour market, return to work after a prolonged absence or contribute to their communities through volunteering roles. While this is clearly the case for unemployed adults, it is also the case for employed adults, and particularly those whose jobs might be at risk of disruption from automation and other megatrends. In Canada, as elsewhere, career guidance for working adults receives less policy attention than career guidance for unemployed adults or for young people. This is a significant gap in the current context of changing demand for skills, when reaching out to workers ahead of job loss is crucial.

This section provides an overview of the system of career guidance for adults in Canada. It sheds light on the main institutions responsible for adult career guidance policy in Canada, how co-ordination is encouraged, who delivers career guidance to adults, and how the services are delivered (e.g. face-to-face or remotely).

Box 1.1. What is career guidance for adults?

This report uses the term 'career guidance' to refer to a range of services intended to assist individuals of all age groups to make well-informed educational, training and occupational choices and to manage their careers. In Canada, career guidance is predominantly known as *career development*, but the terms *career counselling* or *orientation professionelle* are also in use.

Career guidance for adults can be distinguished from career guidance for young people in schools in various ways. First, adults have generally acquired skills through work experience that have not been formally validated. Effective career guidance for adults supports them in identifying employment and training opportunities that leverage these existing skills. Second, career guidance for adults is ideally sensitive to their more complex needs, including childcare and financial responsibilities. Third, having been out of school for longer periods, adults are generally less aware of training opportunities and more familiar with the labour market than are young people, and effective career guidance takes this into account.

There is a growing body of evidence, internationally, to support the claim that career guidance assists adults to strengthen skill development, facilitate labour market transitions and support a better match between the supply and demand of skills and labour (see Box 3.1 in Chapter 3 for a summary). Adults have varying levels of knowledge about labour markets and training opportunities, as well as varying abilities to plan their futures. Career guidance has the potential to level these inequalities and support the labour market inclusion of under-represented groups.

A variety of terminology is used across countries to refer to professionals who deliver career guidance. To retain consistency with previous publications, this report will use the term 'career guidance advisor' to refer to such professionals. In Canada, the term 'career development practitioner' is commonly used, and is generally associated with having received a professional certification.

Source: OECD (2004[28]), *Career Guidance and Public Policy: Bridging The Gap*, https://dx.doi.org/10.1787/9789264105669-en; OECD (2021[29]), *Career Guidance for Adults in a Changing World of Work*, https://doi.org/10.1787/9a94bfad-en.

1.3.1. Responsibility for adult career guidance is shared in Canada

Adult career guidance in Canada is not the responsibility of any one ministry or one level of government. It is embedded in policies relating to employment services and skill development of adults. Employment services, which sometimes include career guidance, are the responsibility of the provinces and territories, which receive financial support from the federal government. Education and training policies, on the other hand, are under provincial mandate. Career guidance relating to upskilling and reskilling of adults, as well as for young people in schools, is therefore primarily a provincial responsibility.

Canadian provinces receive funding from the federal government (through Employment and Social Development Canada, ESDC) to design and deliver employment services under Labour Market Development Agreements (LMDA) and the Workforce Development Agreements (WDA). Career guidance is integrated into a number of employment services that are funded through such agreements. Besides career guidance, other examples of employment services include support in gaining work experience, improving job skills, job search assistance or starting a new business.

With the support of these federal-provincial transfers, Canadian provinces design programming to meet their local labour market needs. Programs and services delivered through LMDAs support Employment Insurance (EI) recipients and those who have paid into EI. Employment services are generally designed by the provincial ministries of labour. In Ontario and Quebec, the provincial public employment service is also involved in designing employment services.

Provincial ministries of education have responsibility for career guidance programmes that support adults in selecting formal adult learning opportunities for upskilling and reskilling. In Ontario, for instance, the Ministry of Education's Prior Learning Assessment and Recognition (PLAR) policy for mature students has components of pathway/career planning embedded within it. The Ontario Ministry of Education's Creating Pathways to Success also offers an education and career planning programme for secondary students, including those who are adult learners. Similarly, career guidance initiatives are a component of Quebec's provincial reskilling programmes (*Programme de l'Aide pour la requalification et l'augmentation de la formation* (PARAF), and *Programme pour la requalification et l'accompagnement en technologies de l'informations et communications* (PRACTIC)).

Neither the federal government nor any of the provinces have a stand-alone career guidance strategy for adults in place. However, four out of the seven provinces in the OECD policy questionnaire (Saskatchewan, British Columbia, Ontario and Quebec) reported having a career guidance strategy for adults that is part of a wider strategy related to employment or the development of skills. This is a common practice in other OECD countries as well. Provided they set out quantifiable targets and timelines, career guidance strategies that are embedded in wider strategies related to employment or skills development can be just as useful as stand-alone strategies. Such strategies can provide much-needed momentum and leadership when they are developed in consultation with relevant stakeholders, and can help to mobilise funding and promote system-wide co-operation.

1.3.2. Co-ordination between stakeholders is encouraged via working groups and information sharing

With responsibility for adult career guidance split between ministries and levels of government in Canada, strong co-ordination is essential to delivering services efficiently and reaching the labour market groups that would most benefit from it. Working groups are the primary means to facilitate federal-provincial co-ordination in Canada, while cross-ministerial co-ordination within provinces is facilitated by a combination of working groups and more informal co-operation. Professional career guidance organisations, like the Canadian Education and Research Institute for Counselling (CERIC) and the Canadian Career Development Foundation (CCDF), support the co-ordination of career guidance. Finally, non-governmental stakeholders engage in career guidance policy in various ways.

A number of working groups support federal-provincial co-ordination on issues related to adult career guidance, including information sharing and discussions about regulating the profession. Co-ordination between provincial-territorial governments and the Government of Canada on labour market issues happens through the Forum of Labour Market Ministers (FLMM) and its working groups. Provincial ministries also engage in bilateral and multilateral ways (through the FLMM) with publicly-funded stakeholders such as the Future Skills Centre and the Labour Market Information Council (LMIC). The LMIC is financed equally by the federal government and the provincial and territorial governments. For instance, provinces share labour market information via a federal/provincial LMI Committee. Moreover, there is co-ordination between the Government of Canada and provinces as part of the Workforce Development Agreements, e.g. the Canada-Saskatchewan Workforce Development Committee. Provinces and territories also co-ordinate together on educational questions through the Council of Ministers of Education, Canada (CMEC), including on issues such as adult learning and foundational skills.

Cross-ministerial co-ordination within provinces is facilitated by a combination of working groups and informal co-operation. In New Brunswick, WorkingNB (the provincial public employment service) is represented on working groups and consulted regularly by the Department of Social Development and Department of Justice and Public Safety. In British Colombia, the Employer and Sector Partnerships branch within the Ministry of Advanced Education and Skills Training develops and maintains partnerships with industry, non-profits, and other government bodies to ensure labour market programming is proactive. In Ontario, there is collaboration between ministries that fund adult education and training services, adult language training services, employment services, and social assistance programs.[3] In Quebec, there is inter-ministerial co-ordination[4] on the development and implementation of national strategies or specific programs affecting the workforce or groups under-represented in the labour market. In Alberta, in addition to involving Alis (Alberta careers, learning and employment information) in steering and working groups, ministries also collaborate informally with one another to complete annual reports, business plans, and Labour Market Transfer Agreement (LMTA) reports.

A number of federal-level career guidance organisations across the country support co-ordination specifically on career guidance, as opposed to employment services or skills development more generally. CERIC is a pan-Canadian charitable organisation that advances education and research on career guidance. Its mission is to build awareness of the benefits of career guidance for social impact, and it does so through advocacy, webinars, an annual conference, and publications. Through its board and advisory committees, CERIC also engages with stakeholders across the country to address shared issues in career guidance. The CCDF is a non-profit centre of innovation and excellence for career guidance policy, research, development, and professional training. For instance, together with Employment and Social development Canada (ESDC), they involved stakeholders nation-wide in the development of a renewed Canadian Competency Framework for Career Development Professionals and a harmonised approach to pan-Canadian professional certification (see Chapter 3). In addition to the above pan-Canadian bodies, some provinces have their own career guidance associations. The Career Development Association of Alberta, for example, provides a free bi-weekly newsletter and hosts an annual conference, which brings together employment and career practitioners, educators, human resource professionals, government staff and employers' and employee organisations.

Other non-governmental stakeholders are involved in various ways. Ontario has adopted a commissioning approach by engaging with external provider organisations, which plan, design and deliver employment services in their respective local areas following an outcome-based approach. These third-party organisations are commissioned to assess the needs of users in a specified area, to design services to meet those needs, and to choose an appropriate delivery mechanism, while making best use of available resources. In Nova Scotia, the Department of Labour and Advanced Education – Skills and Learning Branch also carries out commissioning activities, including launching Market Sounding Exercises to solicit feedback and promote innovation in the employment services delivery model, and holding bilateral meetings with individual vendors about the expected outcomes of the employment services delivery transformation.

Social partners are not explicitly involved in the development of career guidance policies in most provinces, with the exception of Quebec and Nova Scotia. In Quebec, the Labour Market Partners Commission (*La Commission des Partenaires du marchés du Travail*, CPMT) is made up of representatives from trade unions, employer groups, the educational community, community organisations and government agencies. Among other things, it is involved in assuring a good match between available training and the demands of the labour market, by advising the Minister of Labour, Employment and Social Solidarity of Quebec (*Ministre du Travail, de l'Emploi et de la Solidarité sociale).* In Nova Scotia, the public employment service works with employers and with Industry Sector Councils to support employers in building an industry-led approach to human resource development, including the attraction, retention and training of employees.

Overall, the methods used to facilitate co-ordination of career guidance policy in Canada – working groups, information sharing, conferences – are similar to those used in other OECD countries (OECD, 2021[29]), though some countries use additional co-ordination mechanisms. Dedicated bodies in Australia, Ireland, and Norway are involved in co-ordinating career guidance across ministries and levels of government (Box 1.2). The arms-length nature of such bodies, as well as their dedicated budgets and mandate, can make them more impartial than government and effective at engaging stakeholders in policy development and implementation. They do not, however, tend to have power to directly influence policy making on career guidance, such as setting professional standards. In many OECD countries, legislation supports co-ordination by enshrining the right to career guidance into law (OECD, 2021[29]). For instance, Norway recently adopted legislation which requires county municipalities to offer career guidance services to all citizens living in the country, and refugees now have a duty and a right to participate in career guidance when attending an introduction programme.

Box 1.2. International examples of bodies dedicated to co-ordination of career guidance

National Career Institute in Australia

The National Career Institute (NCI) was established in 2019 to ensure that people have access to authoritative and accurate careers information, regardless of their age or employment status. The NCI was originally envisioned as a policy and research body, but has taken on more of an operational role during COVID-19, providing telephone career support to youth. Through its websites (YourCareer.gov.au, Training.gov.au, and myskills.gov.au), NCI disseminates labour market information produced by the National Skills Commission. Both the NCI and the National Skills Commission receive funding through the Australian Government. In addition to disseminating labour market information, the NCI also supports co-ordination through partnership grants, which fund collaborative and innovative career interventions by employers, training providers, schools and community organisations.

National Centre for Guidance in Education in Ireland

The Irish National Centre for Guidance in Education (NCGE) is an agency of the Department of Education. It has responsibility to support and develop high-quality guidance practices in all areas of education (including for adults) and to inform national guidance policy. The centre works with key stakeholders including the public employment service (INTREO), Education Training Boards and schools to provide guidelines, support innovations, organise continuing professional development for career guidance advisors and carry out national surveys on guidance practice and needs. NCGE hosts the National Forum on Guidance twice per year to support communication, co-operation and collaboration across the various guidance sectors in Ireland. It also represents Ireland in discussions at the European Commission about career guidance policy and practice.

Skills Norway

Skills Norway (*Kompetanse Norge*) is the directorate for lifelong learning in Norway in the Norwegian Ministry of Education and Research. Next to skills and adult learning, it is responsible for the strategic leadership of career guidance policy, with the aim of strengthening co-operation and co-ordination among stakeholders, widening access to vulnerable groups, and increasing the quality of lifelong guidance services. Skills Norway established the National Unit for Lifelong Guidance as a national centre to develop and co-ordinate guidance policy and implementation, and to share knowledge and resources. Skills Norway also chairs a National Forum for Career Guidance, the Future Skills Needs Committee, and a number of other expert committees. Skills Norway has recently launched a national digital career guidance service, and developed a national quality framework for career guidance services across sectors.

Source: OECD (2021[29]), *Career Guidance for Adults in a Changing World of Work*, https://doi.org/10.1787/9a94bfad-en; European Commission (2020[30]), "Lifelong guidance policy and practice in the EU: trends, challenges and opportunities", https://op.europa.eu/en/publication-detail/-/publication/4dfac3fa-7a0b-11ea-b75f-01aa75ed71a1/language-en (accessed 9 September 2021).

1.3.3. The most common providers of career services for adults in Canada are government-run employment services and private career guidance services

Comparisons between Canada and other countries in the SCGA must factor in differences in the main survey question. The Canadian version of the SCGA online survey asked adults, "In the past five years, have you used a career service?" This question differs from the question asked of adults in other countries that participated in the survey: "In the past five years, have you spoken to a career guidance advisor?" Career service is a broader term than career guidance. Despite this difference, the rest of the report will draw international comparisons using the online survey data.

The SCGA finds that career guidance in Canada, as in other OECD countries, is delivered by a range of providers (Figure 1.5). Nearly a quarter of adults (24%) report having used a career service through a government-run employment service provider. Another 22% used a private career service, such as a career coach. About 15% of adult users consulted a career service offered through an education and training institution (e.g. school, college, university), while 14% received career services from their employer. Adults also received career service from community-based agencies (12%), business organisations (8%), or trade unions (3%), although these are more minor players. The provider landscape in Canada looks very similar to other OECD countries included in the online survey.

Figure 1.5. Career guidance is delivered by a range of providers in Canada

Share of all adults who used a career service over the past five years, by provider

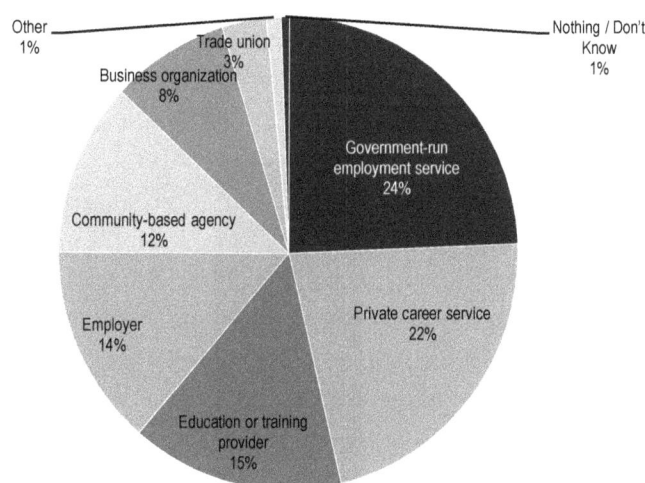

Note: Data refer to the last time the respondent spoke to a career guidance practitioner, and is an average across all provinces and territories in Canada. The repose "other" includes providers such as Website/online career services.
Source: OECD 2020/2021 Survey of Career Guidance for Adults (SCGA).

Government-run employment services

Providing nearly a quarter of all career services, government-run employment services are managed at the provincial level in Canada. Often adults come to these services through another programme, like Social Assistance or Employment Insurance. Government-run employment services are called something different in each province, i.e. Employment Ontario, Nova Scotia Works, WorkBC, Emploi-Québec, Saskatchewan-Canada Career and Employment Service Centres, Alberta Works, Manitoba Jobs & Employment Centres, WorkingNB, Newfoundland and Labrador Employment Centres, and PEI Career Development Centres.[5]

The career services offered by government-run employment services are typically job matching services targeted at unemployed people, rather than career guidance. Job matching has the goal of quickly placing jobseekers into employment. Though career guidance can help jobseekers to find jobs, it ideally takes a more holistic approach where skills, knowledge and abilities are thoroughly assessed, and the individual's motivations and constraints are taken into account when designing career development plans. Unlike job matching, the measure of success of career guidance is not only whether a person finds a job, but could also include any number of milestones towards greater employability and personal well-being: acquiring new skills to manage their career, feeling more positively about their labour market prospects, identifying and/or enrolling in a relevant training opportunity, or acquiring sustainable employment in an occupation they enjoy.

As in other OECD countries, unemployed adults in Canada are more likely to use career services from government-run employment services than are employed adults. The SCGA found that use of career services offered by government-run employment services is higher among the unemployed than among the employed population (Figure 1.6). Still, employed adults in Canada do use government-run employment services, and more so than in other OECD countries. For the most part, government-run employment services are restricted to adults who are eligible for Employment Insurance in Canada, which restricts most employed adults. But there are exceptions – including some government-funded employment programmes in Alberta, New Brunswick, Nova Scotia, Newfoundland and Labrador, and Quebec – where certain types of career services are available to all adults, regardless of employment status.

Figure 1.6. Use of government-run employment services in Canada, by employment status

Share of adult users who received career guidance from the government-run employment services, by employment status

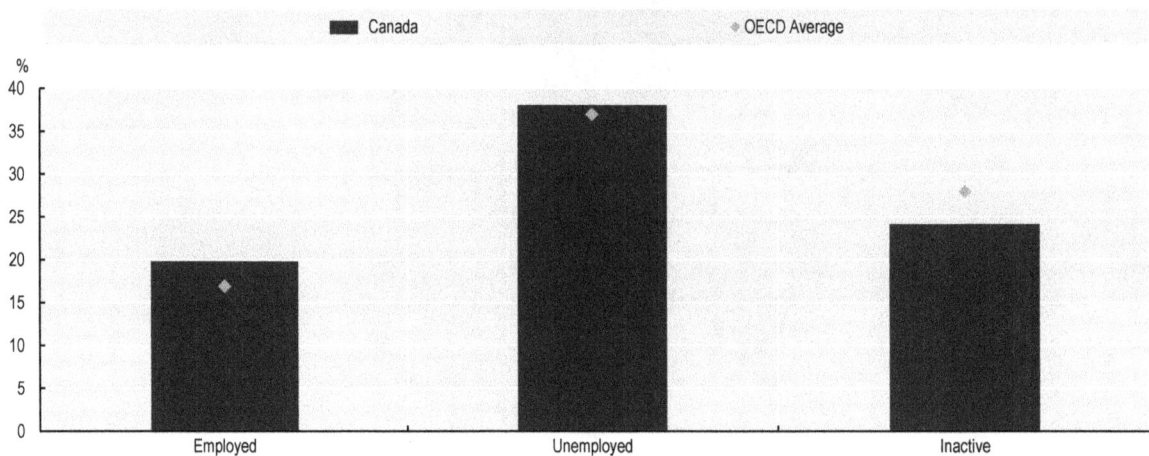

Note: Employment status when the respondent last spoke to a career guidance advisor.
Source: OECD 2020/2021 Survey of Career Guidance for Adults (SCGA).

Expanding public employment services (PES) to employed adults is a common trend across OECD countries, including Austria, Belgium (Flanders), Germany, the Czech Republic, Estonia, Japan, Hungary, Lithuania, and the United States (OECD, 2021[29]). The intention is that expanding the PES to support employed individuals can provide support for impending disruptions. Shifting from a reactive to a more proactive approach requires building the capacity of employment counsellors to serve a broader client base. Germany's public employment service is currently piloting an initiative to build capacity to develop a more proactive and lifelong approach towards career guidance that targets employed workers (Box 1.3). The public employment service in Flanders (Belgium) provides an example of differentiated career services for employed versus unemployed adults (Box 1.3).

Where employed adults are eligible for government-run employment services in some provinces in Canada, they are generally eligible for a narrower set of services than unemployed adults. For instance, employed workers are eligible for employment services through Nova Scotia Works, but support does not include career guidance counselling. Clients are grouped into four streams (A, B, C and D) according to the intensity of the employment barriers they face. Those with the least barriers have access to less intensive support, such as online information, self-assessments or seminars. Such streaming of employment services is common across

OECD countries (including Austria, Greece, the Netherlands and Ireland) and can reduce costs while ensuring that the limited number of employment counsellors spend their time efficiently with adults who have the greatest need. At the same time, this approach also means that employed adults often miss out on access to publicly-subsidised career guidance services.

A common limitation of career guidance provided by public employment services is that it is not well integrated with the adult education and training system. This makes it difficult for employment counsellors at the PES to make good recommendations about training opportunities.

Box 1.3. Extending PES career guidance to employed workers

Germany

As the main provider of career guidance in Germany, the Federal Employment Agency is responsible for delivering guidance services to both young people and adults. For young people, the guidance focuses on their transitions from school to VET, university or work. For adults, the guidance focuses on their transitions from job to job. The 2019 Skills Development Opportunities Act reinforced the entitlement of employed adults to receive free career guidance services through the Federal Employment Agency.

As part of the Lifelong Career Guidance programme (*Lebensbegleitende Berufsberatung, LBB*), the Federal Employment Agency aims to complement current job placement services with career guidance that supports career planning and decision-making over the course of an individual's working life. It also aims to facilitate the up- and re-skilling of adults in order to meet labour market demands.

After a piloting phase, the nation-wide rollout of the programme was in progress at the time of writing, in co-ordination with the relevant ministries at the federal state level. The nationwide rollout included the hiring or retraining of staff to create 450 new LBB advisors in the first three years of the project (2020-22). LBB will not be set up in all local offices, but each labour market region will have a team of 10-20 LBB staff, who can be placed in local offices within the labour market region.

Flanders (Belgium)

The Flemish public employment service (VDAB) facilitates access to career guidance for both unemployed and employed adults. Every citizen, regardless of employment status, can visit the VDAB regional office. Unemployed adults have access to free guidance and training to help them overcome obstacles to employment. Employed and self-employed workers can apply to VDAB for career guidance vouchers, which offer four hours of subsidised career guidance with a mandated career coaching centre of their choice. Individuals have the right to two vouchers (i.e. 8 hours in total) every six years. Consisting of conversations, exercises, and checklists, the career guidance service results in a personal development plan. If training is needed to reach the client's career ambitions, then the career guidance counsellor will help the client identify specific training and inform them about the availability of training vouchers to finance the training.

Source: OECD (2021[31]), *Continuing Education and Training in Germany*, https://doi.org/10.1787/1f552468-en; Dauth et al. (2018[32]), Qualifizierungschancen und Schutz in der Arbeitsversicherung, IAB-Stellungnahme 15/2018, http://doku.iab.de/stellungnahme/2018/sn1518.pdf.

Private providers

About 22% of adult users of career guidance in Canada go through a private provider. Some adults are directed to private providers via the provincial public employment service, which often subcontracts services to private providers (more on the public procurement and accountability systems in Chapter 3). Employed adults who are not eligible for subsidised career guidance via the public employment service, or who do not perceive these services as meeting their needs, may consult private providers of their own initiative. Due to high cost, career guidance delivered by private providers is less accessible to lower-income adults.

Regulating quality among private providers is a challenge. A key issue raised during interviews with Canadian stakeholders is that anybody can call themselves a career guidance advisor or career coach without necessarily having the competences necessary to perform the job. Currently, five provinces out of 13 provinces and territories have a professional certification for career guidance practitioners that is grounded in the Canadian Standards and Guidelines for Career Development Practitioners. To obtain the professional certification, career guidance advisors must demonstrate a combination of relevant education and experience: either a Master's degree in an area related to career development plus one year of work experience in a career development role; or relevant work experience of up to 5 years for those with little or no relevant formal education. Chapter 3 will introduce Canada's federal-level certification initiative developed by the career development profession, and discuss its advantages and disadvantages.

Education or training provider

Some 15% of Canadian adult users reported receiving career guidance from an education or training provider, such as a university or a college. Adult learners may consult career guidance from a university or college when they are considering enrolling in an education or training programme, during the programme itself, and once they've graduated and need support applying what they've learned and progressing in future learning and work.

With education and training being a provincial responsibility, career guidance in education and training institutions is managed either at the provincial, local or institution level. This can result in heterogeneity in the availability and quality of services, which is equally the case across OECD countries.

A benefit of receiving career guidance from an education or training provider is that they can make concrete suggestions about particular training programmes and their availability. A possible disadvantage of career guidance provided by education or training providers, however, is that they may be biased towards recommending programmes that are available at their particular institution. Project GOAL in Europe attempted to overcome this limitation by offering unbiased education guidance at a one-stop service. The idea was that adults could be supported in choosing the most appropriate course among all adult education courses in the country, rather than from only one institution (see Box 2.2 in Chapter 2 for more details).

Employers

Another 14% of adult users reported receiving a career guidance service offered by their employer. In Canada, as elsewhere, few companies offer career guidance services to their employees. Where services are offered, they tend to be outplacement services that employers offer to mitigate legal risks, or focused on key high-potential or "talent" groups, such as the high-qualified or best performers. Large firms are more likely to offer career guidance than smaller firms. Much career guidance offered within firms is job- or company-specific, and focuses on how the individual could progress within the firm, while trying to avoid poaching risks. In Quebec, employers with an annual payroll exceeding CAD 2 million are required by law to invest 1% of their payroll into training activities or else pay into a fund managed by the Labour Market Partners Commission (*La Commission des Partenaires du marchés du Travail,* CPMT), which uses the money to promote employment, adaptation and integration into the workforce, as well as worker mobility.

France and Japan have programmes to encourage more career guidance within firms. These initiatives have the goal of extending career guidance to a wider group of adults, and to support more regular access to career guidance over the course of an employee's career. A common criticism with such programmes is that employers have an interest in keeping the employee within their firm (and managers have an incentive to keep them within their unit), which could undermine the quality of the guidance they provide.

Box 1.4. Public programmes to promote employer-sponsored career guidance

France

The Labour Code in France requires that employers have a professional interview (*entretien professionnel*) every two years with all employees. The mandatory meeting is intended to help the worker consider the prospects for professional development and training.

Japan

In recent years, the Japanese Government has been encouraging companies to offer career guidance to their employees via "self-career docks". With self-career docks, companies set up opportunities for workers to receive regular career consultations throughout their careers. This includes both individual counselling and group counselling in career seminars. Interested employers can receive support in setting up and delivering the self-career docks. For instance, the government commissions nationally certified career counsellors to visit the firm to assist with implementation. Career guidance may be provided by an employee who is a qualified career consultant, by a government-commissioned consultant, or by an external consultant outsourced by the company. Until 2018, employers who introduced the self-career dock system received a government subsidy.

Since 2020, the Japanese Government has set up "Career Development Support Centers" in various parts of the country to promote the use of self-career docks. The Career Development Support Centers hold free introduction seminars for firms, covering topics like how to set up the self-career dock, how frequently to offer guidance, and what content to offer. Consultants from the Career Development Support Center also visit individual companies that are struggling to introduce the system (e.g. SMEs) to provide technical assistance.

Source: OECD (2021[29]), *Career Guidance for Adults in a Changing World of Work*, https://dx.doi.org/10.1787/9a94bfad-en.

Community-based agency

About 12% of employers receive career guidance from a community-based agency. As with private providers, community-based agencies are sometimes subcontracted by the provincial public employment service to offer career guidance services. For instance, Nova Scotia Works, the public employment service in Nova Scotia, consists of 17 community-based employment service providers across the province. Similarly in Quebec, the provincial government subcontracts the delivery of public employment services almost entirely to community-based employment centres. A key advantage of community-based employment service providers is that they are on the ground, can easily make referrals to local resources through their networks, and know the needs of the local population.

Business organisations and trade unions

Delivery of career guidance by business organisations is relatively uncommon in Canada, as elsewhere. Only 8% of Canadian adults receive career guidance from a business organisation (such as the Chamber of Commerce or an Industry Sector Council), which is just above the share in other countries (7% of adults).

The Manitoba Ministry of Education and Training funds the Sector Council Programme, which supports organisations in key sectors to develop and deliver workforce training. Such organisations also inform both youth and adults about jobs and careers in their sector, both in schools and through social media.[6] In Nova Scotia, 15 industry sectors access provincial funding through the Sector Council programme, which supports sector councils to drive an industry-led approach to human resource development. In particular, the programme equips small-and-medium-sized businesses with access to expertise and resources in attracting, retaining and training employees.

Involvement of trade unions in career guidance is low across OECD countries (only 5% of adults use career guidance provided from trade unions), and is particularly low in Canada (only 3% of adults). This partially reflects low and declining union membership among employees across OECD countries, though in many countries, union services depend on coverage in collective bargaining agreements rather than membership.[7] In some OECD countries, trade unions provide career guidance directly. The Icelandic Confederation of Labour has developed an Education and Training Service Centre which co-ordinates the development of career guidance services in co-operation with accredited education providers, and individuals belonging to certain target groups receive free guidance. Unionlearn, which is the learning and skills organisation of the Trade Union Congress in the United Kingdom, has Union Learning Representatives who offer information, advice and guidance, as well as carry out skills assessments and link learners with training.

1.3.4. Face-to-face delivery of career guidance was already less prevalent in Canada prior to the pandemic

According to the SCGA, 25% of adults who received career guidance services in Canada in the last five years received them face-to-face, while 75% used remote alternatives like videoconference (21%), telephone (20%), online chat (18%), instant messaging (16%) or website/online resources (1%) (Table 1.1). Compared to other countries in the survey, Canadians used face-to-face guidance much less (25% versus 54%) and remote alternatives much more (75% versus 46%). This may reflect that face-to-face services are less available in Canada relative to other countries, perhaps due to the geographic challenges of servicing such a large country.

There is a mismatch between how Canadians receive career guidance and how they would prefer to receive it (Table 1.1). In particular, Canadians would prefer to receive more face-to-face service, and less remote service. Close to 40% of Canadian adults said they would prefer to receive career guidance face-to-face (compared to only 25% who did). About 60% said they would prefer remote alternatives (compared to 75% who did).[8] Preferences are very similar across countries.

Table 1.1. Actual and preferred modes of service delivery in Canada and the OECD

Share of adult users of career guidance, by mode of actual and preferred service delivery

	Canada		OECD	
	Actual	Preferred	Actual	Preferred
Face-to-face	24.9	39.1	54.2	43.1
Remote alternatives:	75.1	60.9	45.8	56.9
Videoconference	20.6	7.6	10.3	4.8
Telephone	19.5	9.6	18.4	8.0
Online chat	17.6	8.7	12.0	9.2
Instant messaging	15.6	7.9	4.9	10.3
Website/ online resources	1.1	23.8	-	24.3

Note: The option "website/online resources" was added to the survey for Canada, and was not included for the other countries.
Source: OECD 2020/2021 Survey of Career Guidance for Adults (SCGA).

Remote delivery became even more prevalent in Canada during the pandemic. An international survey of career guidance practitioners sheds light on how service delivery of career guidance adapted during the pandemic (Figure 1.7). Before the pandemic, career guidance services in all countries, including Canada, were generally offered either on-site with some remote services or only on-site, with no remote services. During the pandemic, social distancing requirements made in-person services impossible, and providers had to move towards fully remote delivery. The percentage of respondents in Canada who report that career guidance was delivered fully remotely jumped from 3% prior to the pandemic to 90% during the pandemic. Even after exiting out of lockdowns, respondents predicted that fully and partially remote delivery would be more frequent than before the pandemic. This suggests that there may be a permanent increase in remote delivery even once the economy fully reopens.

Figure 1.7. Career guidance delivery during COVID-19

Share of respondents by main reported delivery channel of career guidance services

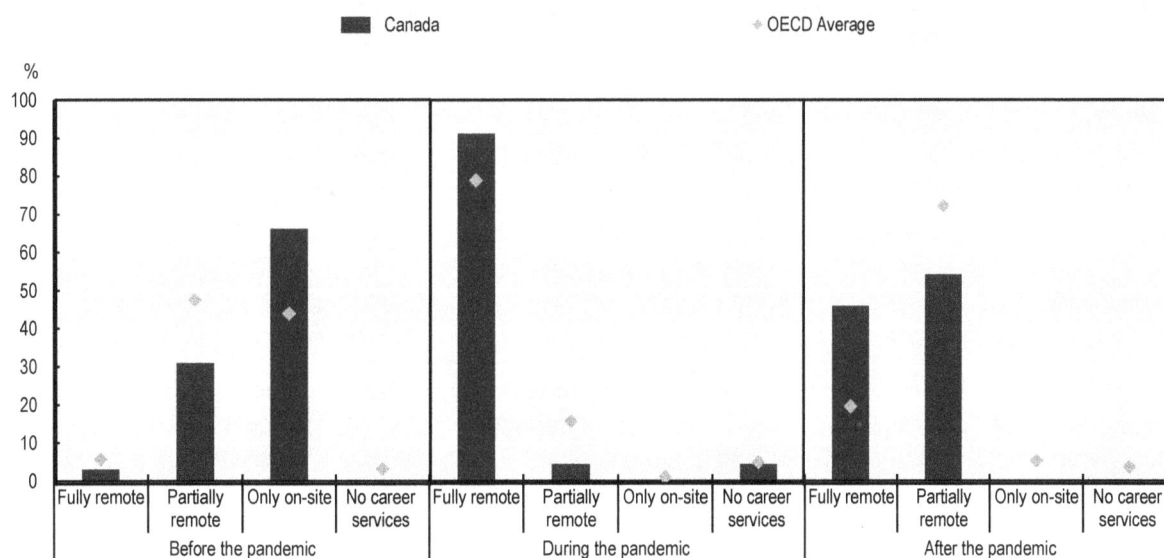

Note: The international survey was conducted in June 2020. Respondents were mainly career guidance practitioners, but also included managers of guidance services, representatives of professional associations or policy officials. Some variation may be due to differences in the timing of policy responses to the pandemic. "After the pandemic" refers to respondents' own projections about how service delivery will change post-pandemic.
Source: Cedefop, European Commission, ETF, ICCDPP, ILO, OECD and UNESCO (2020[33]), *Career Guidance Policy and Practice in the Pandemic. Results of a Joint International Survey*, https://doi.org/10.2801/318103. Based on author's own calculations.

Remote delivery of career services has its advantages and disadvantages. It has the capacity to extend delivery of career guidance to adults living in rural and remote parts of the country, where in-person services may not be available. Indeed, limited access to career guidance in rural and remote regions of Canada was one of the key challenges identified by experts in the OECD policy questionnaire. However, adults in rural and remote regions may lack adequate telephone or internet connections, or the digital skills to be able to use online services effectively. In the OECD policy questionnaire, the Saskatchewan provincial government identified digital literacy as a key challenge to providing career guidance services. Developing tools to assess and develop the digital literacy of clients could support better remote delivery.

Assessment and recommendations

Career guidance for adults has the potential to support the recovery from the pandemic by facilitating employment transitions and reskilling. With responsibility for designing career guidance programmes falling mainly to provinces, this can help to tailor services to meet local needs. That said, there could be a case for more pan-Canadian co-ordination on quality standards, professional certifications, and career guidance legislation.

- Federal, provincial and territorial governments should co-ordinate, possibly through the Forum of Labour Market Ministers or another body designated with this co-ordination role, to develop a strategy for adult career guidance in Canada. Such a strategy, which could be part of wider strategies on adult skill development and/or employment services, could help to mobilise funding and promote system wide co-ordination.

The main providers of career guidance for adults in Canada are provincial government-run employment services, though these tend to focus on the needs of jobseekers, while employed adults are eligible for only a narrow set of services. Expanding service provision to employed adults could more proactively support job transitions.

- Strengthen the capacity of the provincial government-run employment services to create proactive career guidance opportunities for adults in employment at risk of job loss or with poor career prospects.
- Improve co-operation between training providers, government-run employment services and employers with the objective of supporting the provision of impartial career and training guidance for adults.

Canadian adults use face-to-face career guidance considerably less than adults in other countries, despite having a preference for more of this type of service delivery. Remote delivery became even more prevalent during the pandemic, and could potentially extend delivery of career guidance to adults living in rural and remote parts of the country. However, it requires good internet connection and digital skills, and may not be as effective as face-to-face guidance at delivering employment and education outcomes.

- Government-run employment services should continue to offer a mix of face-to-face and remote guidance services, but expand face-to-face provision to meet client demand as sanitary conditions improve.

References

Advisory Council on Economic Growth (2017), *Learning Nation: Equipping Canada's Workforce with Skills for the Future*, https://www.budget.gc.ca/aceg-ccce/pdf/learning-nation-eng.pdf. [20]

Andrews, D. et al. (2020), "The career effects of labour market conditions at entry", *OECD Productivity Working Papers*, No. 20, OECD Publishing, Paris, https://dx.doi.org/10.1787/29c11c75-en. [13]

Bank of Canada (2021), *Our COVID-19 response: Navigating diverse economic impacts*, https://www.bankofcanada.ca/2020/06/our-covid-19-response-navigating-diverse-economic-impacts/ (accessed on 21 July 2021). [7]

Bell, D. and D. Blanchflower (2011), "Young People and the Great Recession", *Oxford Review of Economic Policy*, Vol. 27/2, pp. 241-267, https://www.jstor.org/stable/pdf/43744473.pdf (accessed on 7 February 2022). [14]

Brown, A. et al. (2020), *Lifelong guidance policy and practice in the EU: trends, challenges and opportunities*, European Commission, Publications Office of the European Union, https://data.europa.eu/doi/10.2767/91185. [30]

Caranci, B., F. Fong and Y. El Baba (2021), *Don't Let History Repeat: Canada's Energy Sector Transition and the Potential Impact on Workers*, TD Bank Group, https://economics.td.com/esg-energy-sector (accessed on 28 June 2021). [24]

Cedefop et al. (2020), *Career Guidance Policy and Practice in the Pandemic. Results of a Joint International Survey*, https://doi.org/10.2801/318103. [33]

Dauth, C. et al. (2018), *IAB Stellungnahme Qualifizierungschancen und Schutz in der Arbeitslosenversicherung*, Institut für Arbeitsmarkt- und Berufsforschung, http://doku.iab.de/stellungnahme/2018/sn1518.pdf. [32]

Government of Canada (2021), *Energy and the economy*, Energy and the economy, https://www.nrcan.gc.ca/science-data/data-analysis/energy-data-analysis/energy-facts/energy-and-economy/20062 (accessed on 28 June 2021). [22]

Government of Canada (2020), *Hydrogen Strategy for Canada: Seizing the Opportunities for Hydrogen*, https://www.nrcan.gc.ca/sites/nrcan/files/environment/hydrogen/NRCan_Hydrogen%20Strategy%20for%20Canada%20Dec%2015%202200%20clean_low_accessible.pdf. [23]

Government of Canada and Council of Ministers of Education, Canada (2021), *Adult Learning and Foundational Skills: Findings from the first cycle of the Programme for the International Assessment of Adult Competencies (PIAAC)*, https://www.cmec.ca/Publications/Lists/Publications/Attachments/422/PIAAC_2012_%20Adult_Learning_and_Foundational_Skills_in_Canada_EN.pdf. [26]

ILO (2021), *Skilling, upskilling and reskilling of employees, apprentices & interns during the COVID-19 pandemic. Findings from a global survey of enterprises*, https://www.ilo.org/wcmsp5/groups/public/---ed_emp/---emp_ent/documents/publication/wcms_794569.pdf. [27]

LMIC-CIMT (2021), *Women in Recessions: What Makes COVID-19 Different? LMI Insight Report no. 39,*, https://lmic-cimt.ca/publications-all/lmi-insight-report-no-39/ (accessed on 23 July 2021). [10]

McKinsey Global Institute (2021), *The future of work after COVID-19*, https://www.mckinsey.com/featured-insights/future-of-work/the-future-of-work-after-covid-19 (accessed on 23 January 2022). [15]

Nedelkoska, L. and G. Quintini (2018), "Automation, skills use and training", *OECD Social, Employment and Migration Working Papers*, No. 202, OECD Publishing, Paris, https://dx.doi.org/10.1787/2e2f4eea-en. [19]

OECD (2021), "An assessment of the impact of COVID-19 on job and skills demand using online job vacancy data", *OECD Policy Responses to Coronavirus (COVID-19)*, https://doi.org/10.1787/20fff09e-en (accessed on 3 August 2021). [16]

OECD (2021), *Career Guidance for Adults in a Changing World of Work*, Getting Skills Right, OECD Publishing, Paris, https://dx.doi.org/10.1787/9a94bfad-en. [29]

OECD (2021), *Continuing Education and Training in Germany*, Getting Skills Right, OECD Publishing, Paris, https://dx.doi.org/10.1787/1f552468-en. [31]

OECD (2021), *Labour market statistics. Main Economic Indicators (database)*, https://doi.org/10.1787/data-00046-en (accessed on 22 June 2021). [5]

OECD (2021), *OECD Economic Surveys: Canada 2021*, OECD Publishing, Paris, https://dx.doi.org/10.1787/16e4abc0-en. [1]

OECD (2021), *OECD Employment Outlook 2021: Navigating the COVID-19 Crisis and Recovery*, OECD Publishing, Paris, https://dx.doi.org/10.1787/5a700c4b-en. [12]

OECD (2021), *OECD Labour Force Statistics*, OECD Publishing, Paris, https://dx.doi.org/10.1787/23083387 (accessed on 18 October 2021). [3]

OECD (2020), *Education at a Glance 2020: OECD Indicators*, OECD Publishing, Paris, https://dx.doi.org/10.1787/69096873-en. [11]

OECD (2020), *Preparing for the Future of Work in Canada*, OECD Reviews on Local Job Creation, OECD Publishing, Paris, https://dx.doi.org/10.1787/05c1b185-en. [8]

OECD (2020), *Workforce Innovation to Foster Positive Learning Environments in Canada*, Getting Skills Right, OECD Publishing, Paris, https://dx.doi.org/10.1787/a92cf94d-en. [17]

OECD (2019), *OECD Skills Outlook 2019 : Thriving in a Digital World*, OECD Publishing, Paris, https://dx.doi.org/10.1787/df80bc12-en. [18]

OECD (2019), *The Survey of Adult Skills: Reader's Companion, Third Edition*, OECD Publishing, Paris, https://dx.doi.org/10.1787/f70238c7-en. [25]

OECD (2017), *Pensions at a Glance 2017: OECD and G20 Indicators*, OECD Publishing, Paris, https://dx.doi.org/10.1787/pension_glance-2017-en. [21]

OECD (2004), *Career Guidance and Public Policy: Bridging the Gap*, OECD Publishing, Paris, https://dx.doi.org/10.1787/9789264105669-en. [28]

Statistics Canada (2022), *Gross domestic product (GDP) at basic prices, by industry, monthly*, https://www150.statcan.gc.ca/t1/tbl1/en/tv.action?pid=3610043401 (accessed on 21 January 2022). [6]

Statistics Canada (2022), *Labour Force Survey, December 2021*, https://www150.statcan.gc.ca/n1/daily-quotidien/220107/dq220107a-eng.htm (accessed on 21 January 2022). [4]

Statistics Canada (2021), *COVID-19 in Canada: A One-year Update on Social and Economic Impacts*, https://www150.statcan.gc.ca/n1/pub/11-631-x/11-631-x2021001-eng.htm#a4 (accessed on 23 June 2021). [2]

Statistics Canada (2021), *Labour Force Survey, November 2021*, https://www150.statcan.gc.ca/n1/daily-quotidien/211203/dq211203a-eng.htm (accessed on 23 January 2022). [9]

Notes

[1] Statistics Canada defines long-term unemployment as the share of unemployed people who have been unemployed for 27 weeks or more.

[2] https://www.oecd.org/employment/skills-and-work/adult-learning/dashboard.htm.

[3] Namely, the Ministry of Education, Ministry of Colleges and Universities, Ministry of Labour Training and Skill Development and the Ministry of Children, Community and Social Services.

[4] Le MTESS, le ministère de l'Éducation (ME) et le ministère de l'Enseignement supérieur (MES), le ministère de l'Immigration, de la Francisation et de l'Intégration (MIFI) et le ministère de l'Économie et de l'Innovation (MEI),

[5] OECD Policy Questionnaire and "Federalism in Action: the Devolution of Canada's Public Employment Service 1996-2015."

[6] www.gov.mb.ca/wd/ites/is/associations.html.

[7] According to the OECD Trade Union dataset, 15.8% of employees were members of a union in 2019, down from 20.9% in 2000. In Canada over the same time period, union membership declined from 28.2% to 26.1%.

[8] The sub-group of Canadian adults who received guidance remotely but would have preferred to receive it face-to-face (28% of remote users) did not look significantly different from other users of career guidance in terms of age, gender, education or whether they lived in cities or rural areas.

2 Fostering a greater and more inclusive use of career guidance in Canada

This chapter presents new data on the use of career guidance among adults in Canada, as compared with adults in other OECD countries. It analyses the use of career guidance among different sub-groups of the population, and highlights Canadian and international initiatives to engage greater use of career guidance among under-represented groups. The chapter also covers the reasons why adults seek career guidance in Canada, how usage changed during the COVID-19 pandemic, and the main barriers to greater participation.

Summary

According to the OECD Survey of Career Guidance for Adults, Canadian adults use career guidance much less than their counterparts in other countries. This partly reflects a lower likelihood of using career guidance among the employed population in Canada, relative to other countries in the survey. Adults in Canada are particularly less likely to use career guidance when they want to progress in their current job or when choosing an education or training opportunity. In contrast to other countries, Canadian adults who feel their jobs are at risk of automation are also less likely to consult career services than their peers who do not feel their jobs are at risk.

Use of career guidance among adults increased during the COVID-19 pandemic, particularly among adults who reported that COVID-19 had an impact on their employment status. This is consistent with the fact that most public career guidance is provided to adults through government-run employment services.

Some groups of Canadian adults use career guidance less than others, particularly low-educated adults, older adults and those living in rural areas. With better outreach and targeting of services to the needs of these groups, career guidance could be an important lever to motivate them to train and to improve employability.

The most common reason that adults provided for not using career services was not feeling the need to, and this is in common with other countries in the survey. This was followed by not being aware that services existed. Unlike other countries, however, Canadian adults were more likely to report that they did not have enough time, due to either work or family/childcare responsibilities.

The previous chapter showed how the COVID-19 pandemic had a disproportionate employment impact on vulnerable groups in the labour market, including young people, low-skilled workers, women, temporary employees and Indigenous people. These are some of the same individuals who face higher risk of skills obsolescence and job automation due to technological change. Adult learning can facilitate job transitions during periods of economic instability, but earlier evidence suggests that vulnerable adults who are older, lower-skilled or in low-income jobs tend to participate less in adult learning than their counterparts. To the extent that these gaps are due to a lack of knowledge about adult learning opportunities or their benefits, or to low motivation, career guidance can be an important lever to engage greater participation in adult learning among vulnerable adults. It can also support job transitions and improve employability.

This chapter presents survey evidence on the use of career guidance by adults in Canada, barriers to the use of career guidance, and how inclusive the Canadian system is.

2.1. Use of career guidance services

Adults in Canada appear less likely to consult career guidance advisors than adults in other surveyed countries (Argentina, Brazil, Chile, France, Germany, Italy, Mexico, New Zealand and the United States). According to the SCGA, only 19% of Canadian adults spoke with a career guidance advisor over the past five years. This is nearly half the survey average (39%), and places Canada as the country with the lowest use of adult career guidance services in the survey (Figure 2.1).

While the low use in Canada relative to other countries may be partially due to methodological differences (see Annex B), it is also likely caused by differences in demand and supply factors. On the demand side, adults in Canada are less likely to seek career guidance when they want to progress in their current job or when they are looking for education and training opportunities. This helps to explain why employed adults use career guidance less in Canada (see Figure 2.11 below), which is not the case in other surveyed countries. On the supply side, the survey data does not uncover any glaring issues with the quality of career guidance services in Canada (see Figure 2.8 below). No conclusions could be reached about the adequacy of the supply of career guidance services in Canada based on the survey data.

In addition to using career guidance less, Canadian adults are also less likely than those in other countries to have multiple interactions with a career guidance advisor. Thirty-five percent of Canadian adults reported meeting with their career guidance advisor only once, higher than the average of all countries that participated in the SCGA (25%). This represents a relatively high share of adults not having any follow-up after their initial consultation with a career guidance advisor. That said, 65% of Canadian adults do have follow-up, with 25% of adults meeting with a career guidance advisor twice, 17% three times, and 23% more than three times (compared to 38%, 19% and 18% for the survey average, respectively) (Figure 2.2).

Figure 2.1. Share of adults who have spoken with a career guidance advisor

Share of adults who have spoken with a career guidance advisor over the past five years, by country

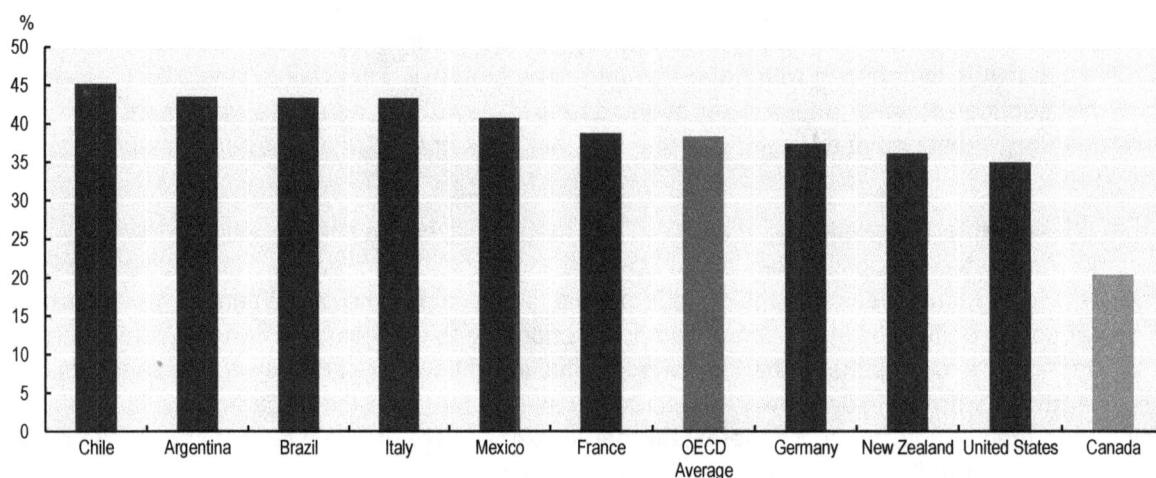

Note: The average includes the 10 countries covered by the SCGA: Argentina, Canada, Chile, Brazil, France, Germany, Italy, Mexico, New Zealand and the United States. In Canada, respondents were asked if they had used a career service in the past five years, while in the other countries respondents were asked if they had spoken with a career guidance advisor over the past five years.
Source: OECD 2020/2021 Survey of Career Guidance for Adults (SCGA).

Figure 2.2. Intensity of use of career guidance services among adults

Share of adults who used career services over the past year, by number of uses/interactions

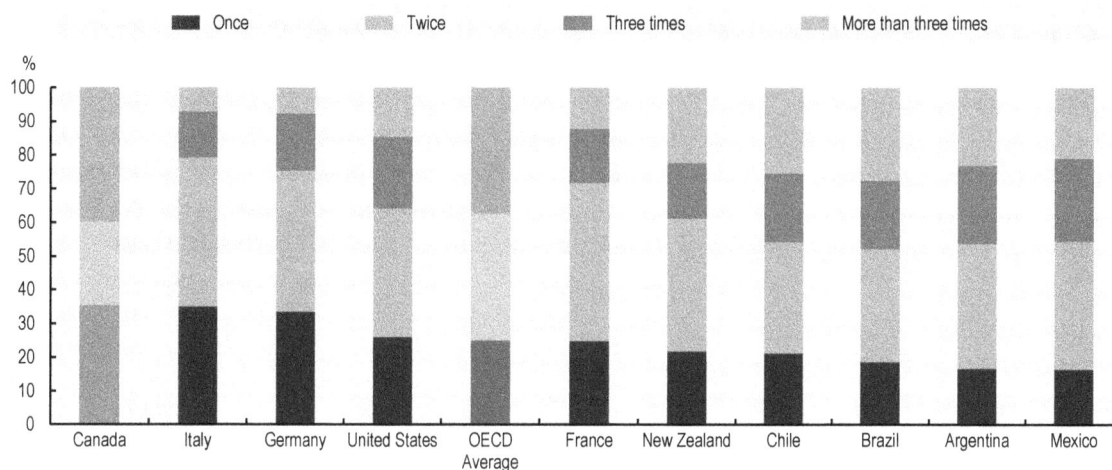

Note: The average includes the 10 countries covered by the SCGA: Argentina, Canada, Chile, Brazil, France, Germany, Italy, Mexico, New Zealand and the United States. In Canada, respondents were asked how many times they used a career service in the last 12 months, while in the other countries respondents were asked how often they interacted with a career guidance advisor over the past 12 months.
Source: OECD 2020/2021 Survey of Career Guidance for Adults (SCGA).

Figure 2.3. Reasons for seeking career services, Canada and OECD average

Share of adults who used career services over the past five years, by reason

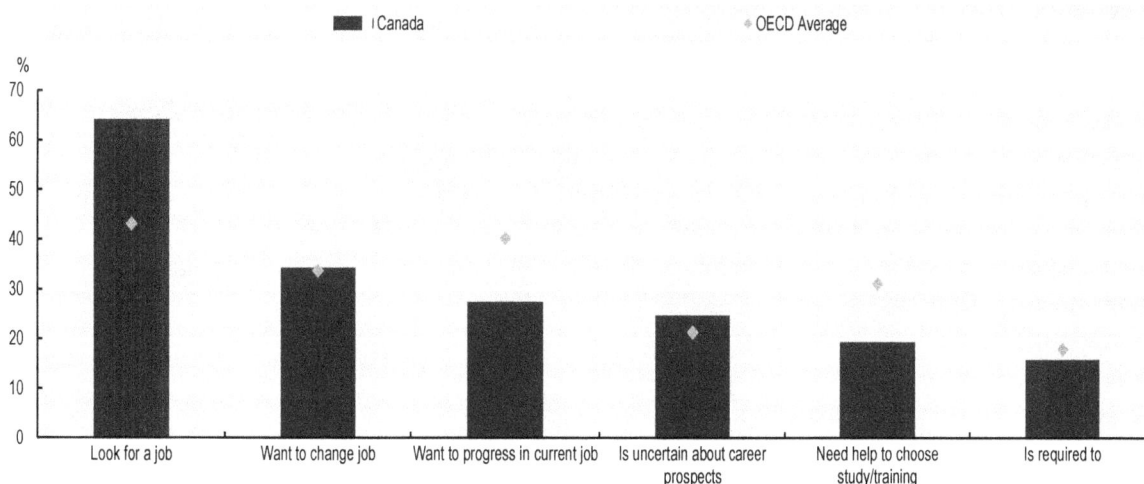

Note: The average includes the 10 countries covered by the SCGA: Argentina, Canada, Chile, Brazil, France, Germany, Italy, Mexico, New Zealand and the United States. Respondents could choose more than one answer. Data refers to the last time the respondent spoke to a career guidance advisor / used career services. In Canada, respondents were asked about their reasons for using career services, while in the other countries, respondents were asked about their reasons for speaking to a career guidance advisor.
Source: OECD 2020 Survey of Career Guidance for Adults (SCGA).

Canadian adults also have different reasons for using career services compared to adults in other OECD countries (Figure 2.3). The majority of Canadian adult users (64%) consulted career services to find a job, a much higher share than observed on average across countries (43%). Contrary to what one might think, these adults are not all unemployed: in fact, 56% of adults who say they spoke with a career guidance advisor to find a job were employed at the time they received guidance. They were either looking to change jobs or looking for a second or third job. Only 28% were unemployed and 16% were not active in the labour force. Canadian adults are less likely than their international counterparts to seek guidance when they are choosing a study or training programme (19% versus 31%), or when they want to progress in their current job (27% versus 40%).

2.1.1. Adults in Canada use other types of career support less than those in other countries

One possibility for the low rate of career guidance usage in Canada could be that Canadians prefer other types of career support, like consulting career information online, speaking with friends and family, or participating in career development activities like information interviews or work visits. However, a look at the survey data in international comparison suggests that adults in Canada also use these alternative sources of career support less than their international counterparts.

Figure 2.4 shows the use of online information in international comparison. Just over half of Canadian adults (53%) reported that they looked online for employment, education and training opportunities over the past 5 years. This is a lower share than the OECD average (69%). Older adults use online information less than prime-aged adults (37% versus 58%), which is not surprising given that older adults tend to have lower digital skills and are also less likely to be looking for new jobs. Adults in rural areas also report a lower use of online information compared to adults in urban areas (43% versus 55%); likely related to inferior broadband access in rural versus urban areas in Canada. Finally, there are also gaps in the use of online information by education level: lower-educated adults, too, use online information less than high-educated adults (48% versus 66%).

Canadian adults are also less likely than their international counterparts to participate in career development activities (Figure 2.5). Fifty-five (55%) per cent of adults in Canada reported that they had not participated in any type of career development activity in the 12 months preceding the survey. This compares with 42% of adults on average for all countries participating in the SCGA. The most common type of career development activity that Canadian adults did was speak to a family member or friend about training or employment possibilities (22%), followed by discuss career development with a manager or HR professional at work (10%), do an information interview (9%), visit a job fair (7%), and participate in a job rotation/work visit (6%).

Figure 2.4. Use of online information in international comparison

Share of adults who looked online for information on employment, education and training opportunities over the past five years

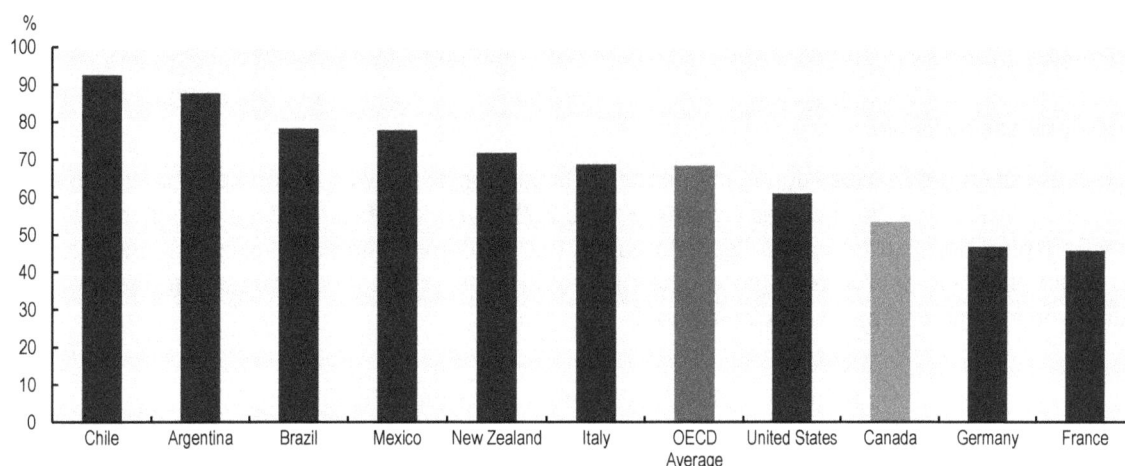

Note: The average includes the 10 countries covered by the SCGA: Argentina, Canada, Chile, Brazil, France, Germany, Italy, Mexico, New Zealand and the United States.
Source: OECD 2020/2021 Survey of Career Guidance for Adults (SCGA).

Figure 2.5. Participation in other career development activities, Canada and OECD average

Share of adults reporting to have carried out career development activities over the past 12 months, by type

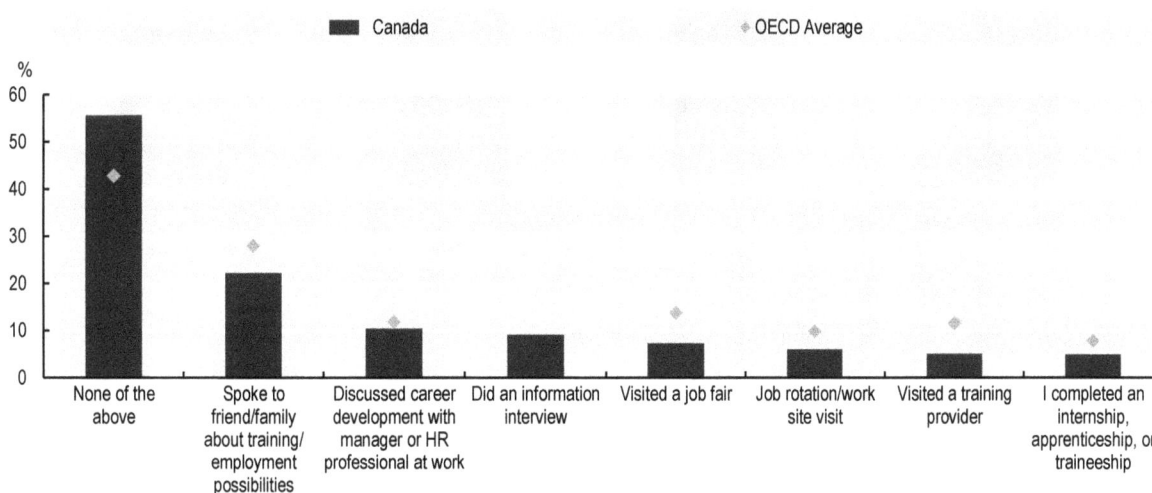

Note: Only the Canadian survey included "did an information interview" as a response option. Average includes Argentina, Brazil, Chile, Canada, France, Germany, Italy, Mexico, New Zealand and the United States.
Source: OECD 2020/2021 Survey of Career Guidance for Adults (SCGA).

2.1.2. Adults in Canada increased their use of career guidance during COVID-19

Evidence from the SCGA suggests that Canadians increased their use of career services during the COVID-19 crisis, likely in response to the spike in unemployment rates and a reduction in hours worked. Among adults who said they used career guidance over the past five years, the large majority (68%)

reported that COVID-19 had had an impact on their employment. This is a much higher share than reported among non-users of career guidance (39%), and suggests that adults may have sought career guidance during this moment of economic instability to help them to navigate the changing labour market.

Adults who reported that COVID-19 had an impact on their employment were also more likely to expect to use career guidance as much or more in the next 12 months. According to survey results, 44% of adults reported using career services more often than before the pandemic to navigate ongoing changes in the labour market (Figure 2.6). Only 22% said that they used career services less because digital or in-person services were less available.

The rise in use of career services during the pandemic is corroborated by an international survey of career development practitioners that included Canada (Figure 2.7). Over half of career development practitioners observed a higher demand for career services during the pandemic, and specifically demand for labour market information, job search assistance, short information delivery chats, requests for information on education and training and psychosocial support.

Figure 2.6. Change in the use of career guidance services during COVID-19, Canada

Share of adults reporting a change in behaviour related to career guidance in response to COVID-19 and its mitigation measures

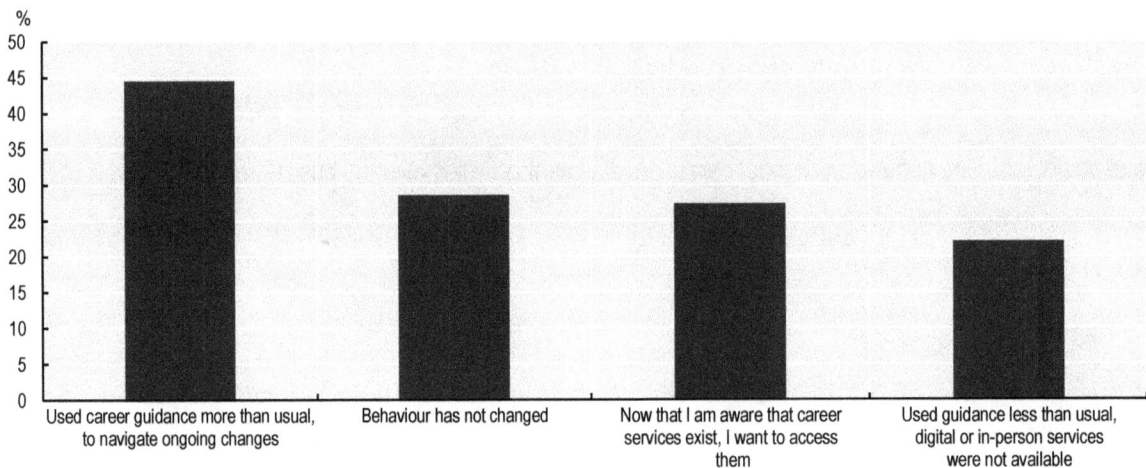

Note: Respondents could choose more than one answer.
Source: OECD 2020/2021 Survey of Career Guidance for Adults (SCGA).

Figure 2.7. Reported increase in demand for career guidance during the pandemic, Canada and OECD average

Percentage of respondents who agree or strongly agree with the following statement

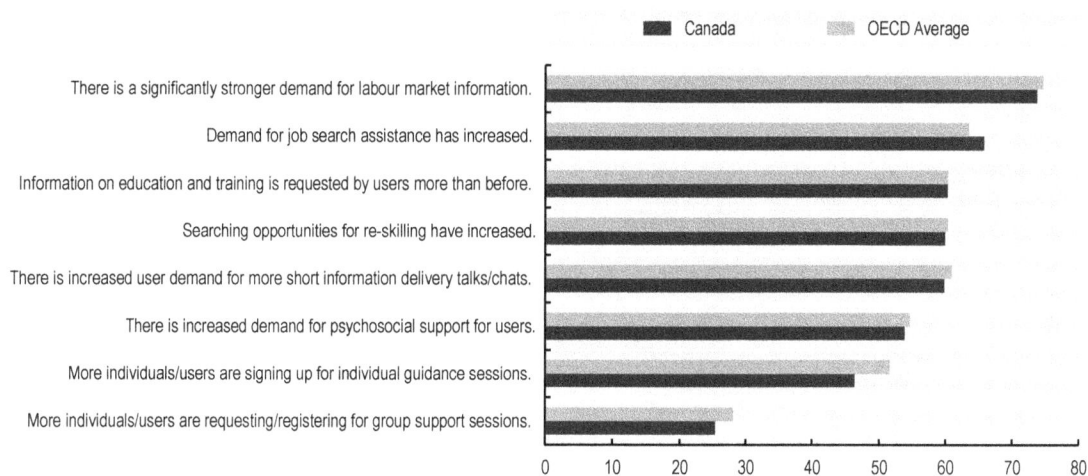

Note: Respondents are mainly career guidance advisors, but also include managers of guidance services, representatives of professional associations or policy officials across Canada. Due to limited sample size in some countries, the OECD average shown here is not an average of individual country averages, but the average of all survey responses in OECD countries. The number of responses per country varies. Source: Cedefop, European Commission, ETF, ICCDPP, ILO, OECD and UNESCO (2020[1]), Career Guidance Policy and Practice in the Pandemic. Results of a Joint International Survey, https://data.europa.eu/doi/10.2801/318103. Based on author's own calculations.

2.1.3. Barriers to accessing career guidance services include not feeling the need to, and not being aware

Understanding the reasons why Canadian adults do not use career services could spark thinking about how coverage and inclusion might be improved. The most common reason reported was simply not feeling the need to use career guidance services (49%) (Figure 2.8), a share that is on par with the average in other surveyed countries (50%). These adults may be well positioned in their careers or perhaps they are unconvinced about the benefits of career development. Unemployed adults were more likely to report not feeling a need to use career services than were employed adults (66% versus 51%). This pattern is similar in other countries in the survey, where 62% of unemployed and 44% of employed adults reported not feeling a need to use career services.

Figure 2.8. Reasons for not using career services, Canada and OECD average

Share of adults who did not use career services over the past five years, by reason

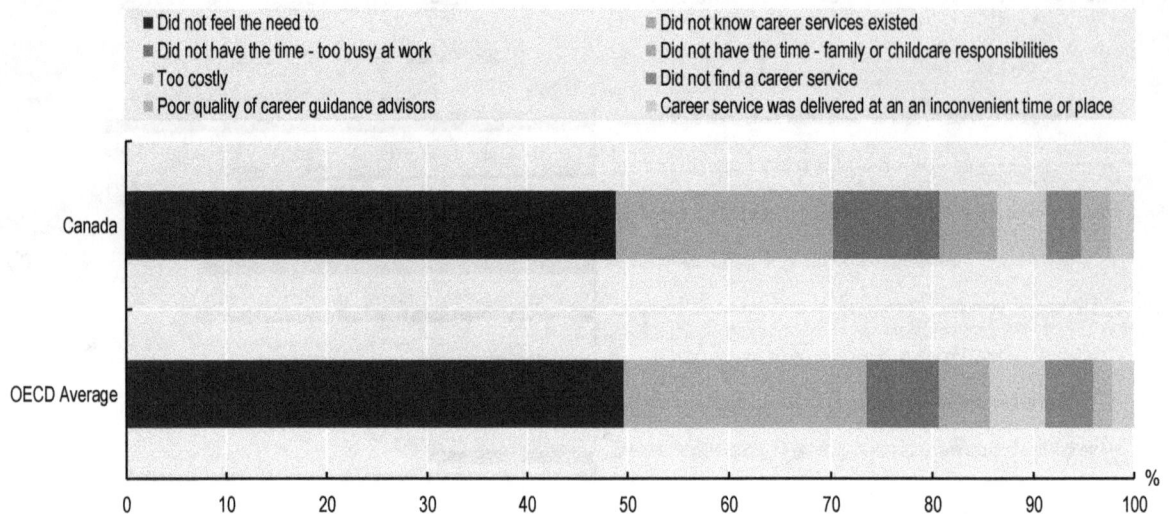

Note: The average includes the 10 countries covered by the SCGA: Argentina, Canada, Chile, Brazil, France, Germany, Italy, Mexico, New Zealand and the United States. Respondents in Canada were asked why they did not use career services, while respondents in the rest of the countries covered by the survey were asked about why they had not spoken to a career guidance advisor.
Source: OECD 2020/2021 Survey of Career Guidance for Adults (SCGA).

The next most common reason for not using career guidance was not being aware that services existed (21%), followed by not having enough time due to work responsibilities (10%) or family or childcare responsibilities (6%). The share of adults who reported not having enough time as a key barrier was higher in Canada relative to the survey average (16% versus 12%). Relatively few respondents complained that services were too costly (5%), not available (3%), of poor quality (3%), or delivered at an inconvenient time or place (2%).

Raising awareness about career guidance services in Canada and finding ways to make consulting a career guidance advisor more compatible with work and family responsibilities could help to improve take-up of services by addressing barriers related to lack of awareness and lack of time. National media campaigns, like the 2020 'En alles beweegt' ('And everything is moving') campaign in Flanders (Belgium), could help to raise awareness about the availability and value of career guidance services. Another way to raise awareness is through referrals between public services. If existing employment, social and adult education services are well connected, adults are more likely to learn about career guidance opportunities. In Ontario, there are multiple entry points for adults to enter adult education opportunities – such as through Employment Service and Literacy and Basic Skills service providers, school boards, Co-ordinated Language Assessment and Referral System Centres – and each provides an opportunity to be referred to career guidance.

The fact that cost is not a major barrier to accessing career guidance in Canada is positive and substantiated by the high share of adults who receive services for free (Figure 2.9). Less than one-third (31%) of adults paid out-of-pocket for the career services they received. The remaining 69% reported receiving career services for free. Adults paying out-of-pocket in Canada represent a higher share than in European countries in the survey (France, Germany, Italy), but this share is on par with the overall average across countries in the survey. Subsidised career services are often made available to adults participating in social programs with a labour market integration component. Indeed, some 55% of adults using career services reported receiving additional income from one or more of the following social programs: Employment Insurance (27%), Social Assistance (20%), Canadian Emergency Response Benefit (12%), or Refugee Support (6%) (Figure 2.10). This reflects that participation in social programs is an important channel through which adults are referred to career services in Canada.

Figure 2.9. Adults' financial contribution to career guidance

Share of adult career guidance users who paid (partially or fully) for services

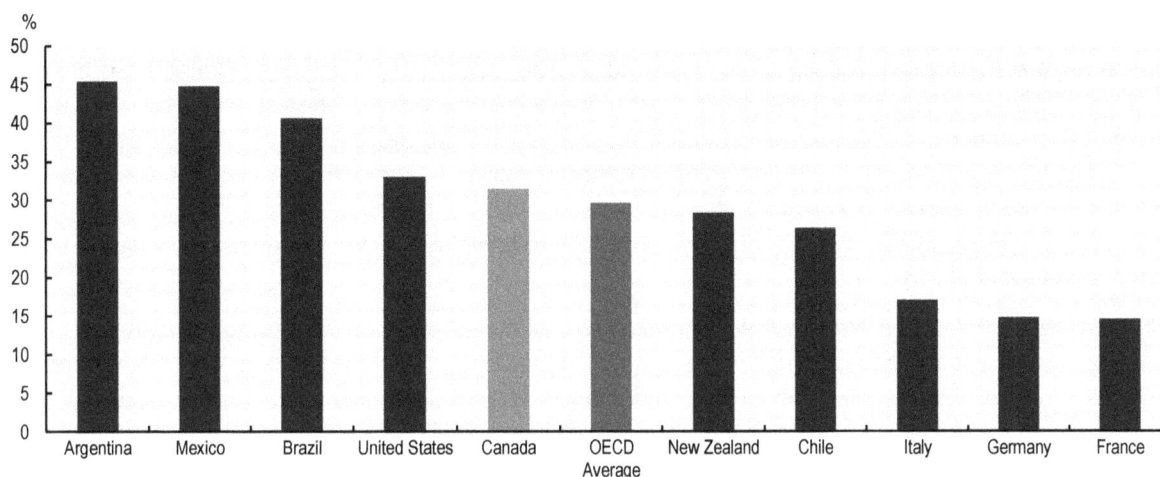

Note: The average includes the 10 countries covered by the SCGA: Argentina, Canada, Chile, Brazil, France, Germany, Italy, Mexico, New Zealand and the United States. Data refer to the last time the respondent used a career service (in the case of Canada) or spoke to a career guidance advisor (for all other countries).
Source: OECD 2020/2021 Survey of Career Guidance for Adults (SCGA).

Figure 2.10. Beneficiaries of additional income support, Canada

Share of adults reporting that they were receiving income from any of the following programmes when accessing career services

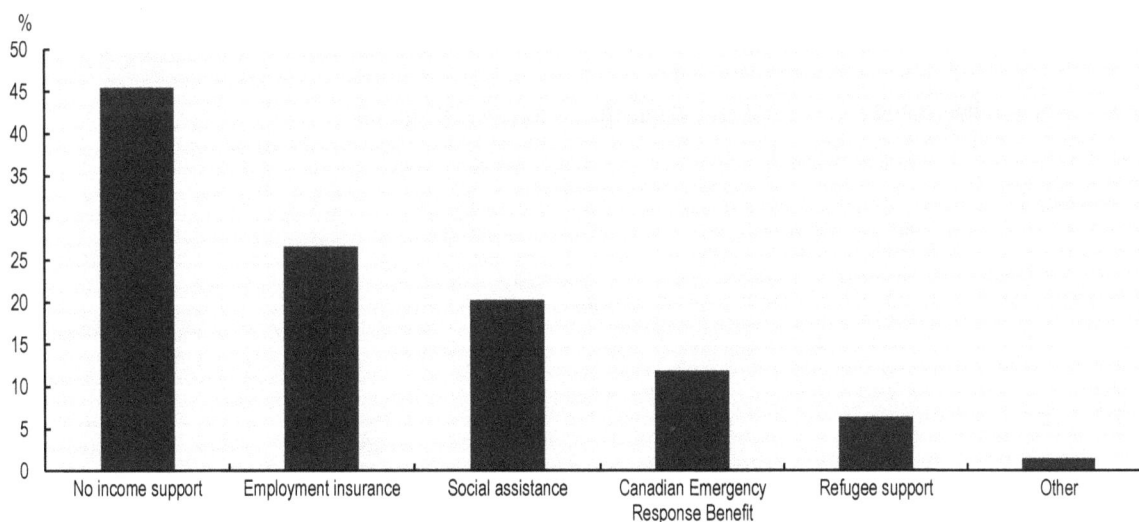

Note: Respondents could choose more than one answer. Data refers to the last time the respondent used career services.
Source: OECD 2020/2021 Survey of Career Guidance for Adults (SCGA).

2.2. Inclusiveness of career guidance services

Not all Canadian adults use career guidance services equally (Figure 2.11). Some groups are much less likely to use career services, including low-educated adults (17% versus 29% for highly-educated adults), older adults

(10% versus 24% for prime-aged adults) and those living in rural areas (14% versus 21% for adults living in cities). Women also use career guidance less than men (18% versus 23%). The use of career guidance among immigrants is higher than among the native-born population in Canada (27% versus 17%), possibly reflecting Canada's targeted services to support the labour market integration of immigrants. Part-time employed use career guidance more than full-time employed (28% versus 23%), and unemployed adults in Canada use career guidance more than employed adults (27% versus 23%). This latter result is unique to Canada. On average across the countries in the survey, employed and unemployed use career guidance equally. The lower use of career guidance among employed adults in Canada may reflect that they are less likely to seek career guidance when looking for education or training opportunities or to progress in their job (Figure 2.3). Table 2.1 presents results from a probit regression which isolates the impact of each of the above factors on the use of career guidance. All relationships from the descriptive analysis above continue to hold, though the explanatory power of the model is very low.

Adults who feel that their jobs are at risk are unfortunately not more likely to consult career guidance services in Canada, in contrast to other countries in the survey (Figure 2.12). Less than 10% of adults who reported feeling "negative" or "very negative" about their future labour market prospects sought career guidance. This contrasts with 40% of adults who reported feeling "positive", and with 22% of adults who reported feeling "very positive." This pattern differs markedly from that of other countries in the survey, where adults who were most worried about their career prospects were more proactive in participating in career guidance. Since adults whose jobs are at risk, or could be in the future, could arguably benefit the most from career guidance, this is an area to investigate and address.

There are also regional differences in the use of career guidance among adults. Across Canada, adults in Ontario use career guidance the most (23%), while those in the Atlantic provinces and Quebec use career guidance slightly less than the Canadian average (18% and 17%, respectively). British Colombia and the Prairie provinces all had participation rates close to the Canadian average of 19%. This might reflect that services in Ontario are available to wider groups of people than in other parts of Canada.

Figure 2.11. Use of career guidance services, by socio-economic and demographic characteristics, Canada

Share of adults who have used career services over the past five years, by group

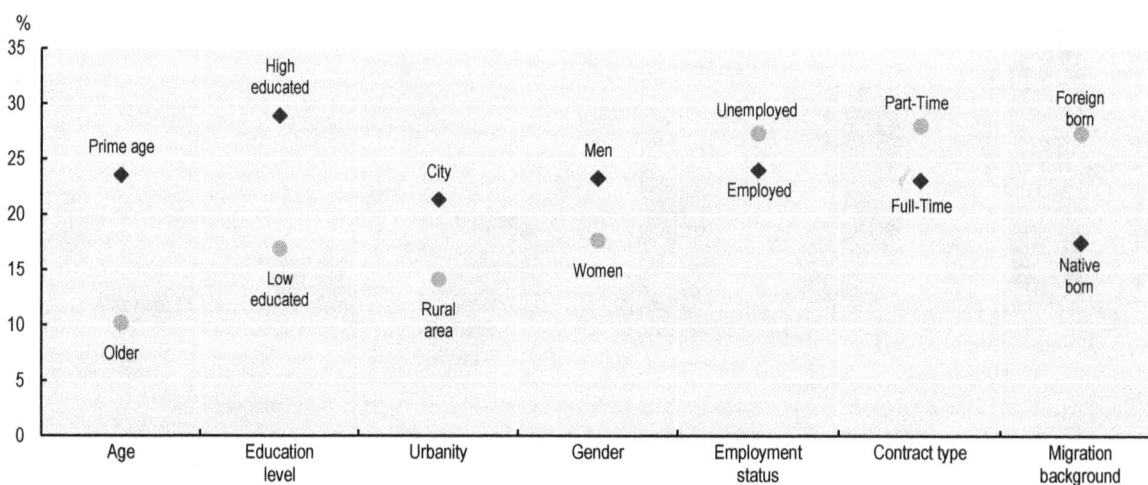

Note: The low educated group includes adults with a low or medium level of education (i.e. less than a bachelor's degree). Prime age refers to adults aged 25-54, and older to adults aged 54 or more.
Source: OECD 2020/2021 Survey of Career Guidance for Adults (SCGA).

Table 2.1. Use of career guidance services, by socio-demographic and demographic characteristics, Canada

Marginal effects from a probit regression

	All respondents	
Age (ref=25-54)		
>54	-0.113	***
Place of residence (ref=Urban)		
Rural Area	-0.042	**
Education (ref=Low-educated)		
Highly-educated	0.076	***
Gender (ref=Men)		
Women	-0.040	***
Employment status (ref=Employed)		
Unemployed	0.048	**
Inactive	-0.101	***
Migration (ref="foreign" born)		
Native born	-0.060	***
Pseudo R^2	0.062	
Observations	3563	

Note: Robust standard errors in parentheses: *** p<0.01, ** p<0.05, * p<0.1. The table reports marginal effects, i.e. percentage change in the outcome variable following a change in the relevant explanatory variable. Marginal effects for categorical variables refer to a discrete change from the base level. For some variables, some categories are not shown in the table.
Source: OECD 2020/2021 Survey of Career Guidance for Adults (SCGA).

Figure 2.12. Use of career guidance services among adults, at different levels of confidence about future labour market prospects, Canada

Share of adults who used career services over the past five years, by level of confidence about future labour market prospects

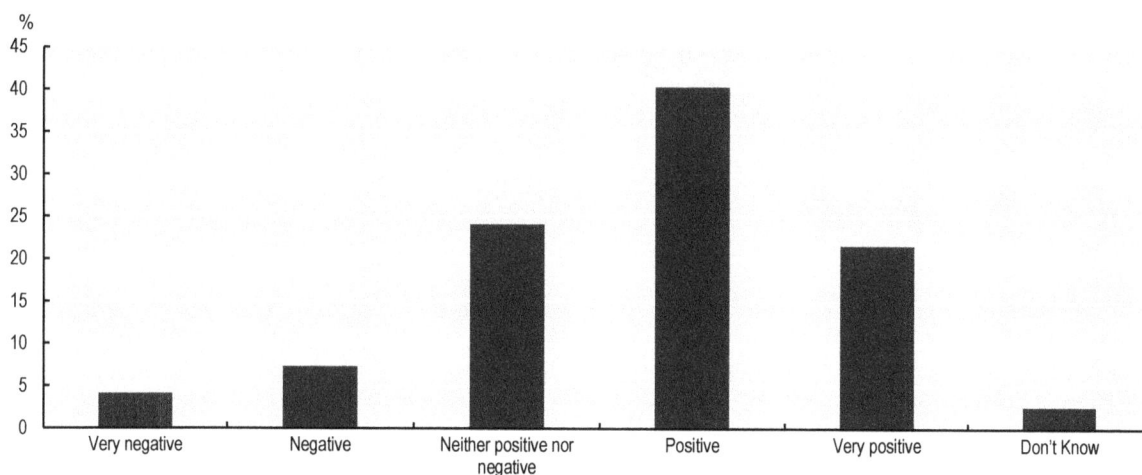

Source: OECD 2020/2021 Survey of Career Guidance for Adults (SCGA).

2.2.1. Active outreach can support greater use of career guidance by under-represented groups

Adults who use career guidance less already face challenges in the labour market. Older, low-educated adults and those living in rural areas tend to participate in training less than their counterparts do (Figure 2.11). They also face greater challenges in accessing employment opportunities. Adults who feel negatively about their future labour market prospects are also less likely to use career guidance services, suggesting that they may not be aware that such services exist, or that services do not meet their needs. With better outreach, career guidance could motivate and support these adults to access training and employment opportunities.

While Canada has dedicated funding to support the labour market integration of under-represented groups, there is little in the way of active outreach. All seven provinces that responded to the OECD policy questionnaire reported that they have policies or programmes in place to target disadvantaged groups and support their access to career development services. For the most part, this refers to earmarked funding for employment services for specific groups under the federal-provincial transfer payment agreements. For instance, the WDAs allocate specific funding to employment and training supports for persons with disabilities, as does the federal Opportunities Fund for Persons with Disabilities. Provinces also reported applying a Gender Based Analysis (GBA+) lens to new employment services programmes, which involves considering how diverse groups of people may experience new programmes. However, no province mentioned having programmes in place to actively reach out to vulnerable adults in the community to connect them with career guidance services.

International examples shed light on possible outreach methods. Jobs Victoria Advocates is an Australian programme that has "advocates" reach out to vulnerable groups in the community to connect them with employment services, including career guidance. Advocates connect with adults where they already are: libraries, community centres, public housing foyers, shopping centres and other community services. In some cases, they even make door-to-door visits. As an alternative approach, facilitators of the Guidance and Orientation for Adult Learners (GOAL) project in Europe built partnerships with community organisations that provided them with referrals to potentially vulnerable adults (Box 2.1). In the Netherlands, the trade union CNV offers career guidance services to its members through *James Loopbahn* (James Career) and trained "Learning Ambassadors" are tasked with reaching out to lower-educated adults or those who might be at risk of losing their job to connect them with guidance and training.

Box 2.1. Outreach to low-educated adults to participate in career guidance

Project GOAL – Guidance and Orientation for Adult Learners

The hypothesis underpinning Project GOAL was that an independent one-stop guidance service that focuses on the specific needs of low-educated adults could increase the participation of this group in adult learning.

Six European countries piloted new guidance models as part of this project: Belgium (Flanders), the Czech Republic, Iceland, Lithuania, the Netherlands, and Slovenia. While each programme sought to develop a guidance model suited to the respective country's potential clients, there were a number of shared practices: guidance services that were one-to-one and face-to-face, unbiased (i.e. not promoting courses offered at only one given educational institution), tailored, empowering, and informative.

Outreach activities to identify and attract low-educated adults to GOAL were an important part of the programme. Most countries achieved their service user recruitment targets through referrals from partner organisations. Building these partnerships required a lot of time and effort, as did building relationships with the adults themselves.

Lack of knowledge about educational opportunities was found to be a key barrier to training, and the GOAL programme filled this knowledge gap. Based on surveys 2-4 months after the programme ended, 38% of participants reported that they had fully achieved their educational goals and an additional 50% said they had made some progress towards these goals. Among those who had entered the programme to pursue educational (as opposed to employment) objectives, 71% had enrolled in a course.

Some caveats were noted. First, education guidance may not be a sensible investment for governments in the absence of free or subsidised adult education courses that clients can progress into. Second, building partnerships with community organisations was necessary to secure participation of low-educated adults in the programme, and this proved to be more costly and to require more effort the more vulnerable or hard-to-reach the potential client was.

Source: Carpentieri et al. (2018[2]). "Guidance and Orientation for Adult Learners: Final cross-country evaluation report", https://adultguidance.eu/images/Reports/GOAL_final_cross-country_evaluation_report.pdf.

2.2.2. Targeting services to the specific needs of vulnerable groups can also improve inclusiveness

Another way to improve the inclusiveness of the adult career guidance system is by better targeting services to the specific needs of vulnerable groups. Compared to delivering career guidance to young people, delivering career guidance to adults can be more challenging because adults tend to have more complex needs, including the need to support a family. Policy questionnaire responses indicate that providing career guidance to adults with low literacy, numeracy or digital literacy is a particular challenge.

Many career guidance services in Canada are designed for particular groups, including Indigenous people, people with disabilities, and newcomers to Canada. For instance, British Colombia's Career Paths for Skilled Immigrants programme offers skilled newcomers career guidance, as well as financial support for language training, assessment of credentials and experience, and support in getting foreign credentials recognised in Canada. In Nova Scotia, the public employment service has agreements with third-party organisations to provide employability and technical skills training, work experience and jobs in IT for under-represented groups in the workforce, including visible minorities.

During interviews, several experts identified Indigenous groups as a vulnerable population that could be better served by career guidance. Experts stressed that services for Indigenous groups require a partnership approach, whereby the services are designed in partnership with community leaders. By marrying the traditional Indigenous advice-giving approach with insights and experience from the professional career services, the hope is that Indigenous adults could be better served. A qualitative study on Indigenous adult women in Quebec finds, for example, that career guidance was successful in supporting the attainment of educational and career goals when career guidance advisors were sensitive to and aware of the complex barriers to employment faced by this group (Joncas and Pilote, 2021[3]). The People and Communities in Motion programme in Quebec provides an example of a programme aimed at improving the employability of adults facing multiple complex barriers by establishing year-long client-counsellor relationships and targeting services to the unique needs of the client (Box 2.2).

Offering career guidance programmes that are well-tailored to the needs of particular groups requires sufficient and consistent funding. In the policy questionnaire, several provinces noted that additional resources would support career development for under-represented adults. For instance, Saskatchewan's Ministry of Immigration and Career Training called for funding to support further skill and career enhancement for older workers, and particularly to develop assessment tools to track their skills and to facilitate their access to training. Alberta[1] emphasised the need for funding to develop specialised assessment and career planning tools, including pre-employment assessments for Indigenous groups. Nova Scotia's Labour and Advanced Education Ministry expressed the need for funding to carry out longer-term evaluations of career guidance programmes for low-skilled and low-qualified adults, recognising that labour force attachment of these groups is a longer-term investment.

Box 2.2. People and Communities in Motion – Quebec

The Quebec Government commissioned a study to understand the effectiveness of People and Communities in Motion (PCM), a 12-month career guidance programme which aims to improve employability of long-term unemployed adults who have many and complex barriers to employment. The programme took place in nine communities in Quebec between 2008 and 2010. During the programme, participants received financial support to cover childcare and transport costs.

The PCM approach follows an open framework that allows for flexibility and targeting services to the unique needs of the individual. Common factors include a year-long commitment that generally involves a series of informal group activities or individual career guidance meetings. Innovative aspects of PCM include locating services within local community centres, close to where the adult lives, as well as its strong emphasis on participation in community projects and a mobilisation of key community resources. At the end of the community project, participants engaged in a skills assessment (*bilan de compétences*), which aimed to validate both the skills they had acquired through the community project and in their previous experience. Following this, they received group guidance towards achieving their educational and employment objectives.

The study found a number of positive impacts from the programme, including higher self-esteem, sense of self-efficacy related to succeeding in work or a training programme, perception of social support, motivation to work and a decrease in negative emotions. Over the course of the programme, the majority of participants entered employment, internships, studies or volunteer work. The relationships created during the community project facilitated the movement of participants towards work or education. The average number of months on social assistance also decreased, and many participants reported less feelings of social isolation as a result of the programme. In some groups, lifestyle improvements were observed in use of drugs and alcohol, diet, and fitness. The study also noted impacts on the counsellors and facilitators; notably, a newfound appreciation for the complexities of the obstacles that participants encounter in their life contexts.

Source: Michaud, G. et al. (2012[4]), *Développement d'une approche visant à mobiliser la clientéle dite éloignée du marché du travail*, http://bv.cdeacf.ca/EA_PDF/161000.pdf.

Assessment and recommendations

Survey data suggests that Canadian adults use career guidance much less than their counterparts in other countries, particularly when choosing an education or training opportunity or when they want to progress in their current job. The most common reasons reported for not using career guidance were not feeling a need for the services, and not being aware that services existed – but these shares of non-users were comparable to those in other surveyed countries. Canada had a higher share of adults reporting not having enough time due to work or childcare/family responsibilities as the main reason they did not use career guidance.

- To raise awareness about career guidance services, provinces and territories could strengthen referrals between public services and launch a media campaign to draw attention to the availability of career guidance opportunities and their value.

As noted in Chapter 1, governments should strengthen the capacity of the provincial government-run employment services to create proactive career guidance opportunities for adults in employment. Also, better co-operation between training providers, government-run employment services and employers would support greater participation in career and training guidance for adults.

More could be done to engage under-represented adults in career guidance, in particular vulnerable groups such as low-educated, older adults and those living in rural areas. These adults are both less likely to use traditional career services and to search online for information about employment and training opportunities. In contrast to adults in other countries, adults in Canada who feel that their jobs are at risk are less likely to consult career guidance services than their peers who are less at risk. Lessons from the GOAL project in Europe and Quebec's People and Communities in Motion pilot suggest that engaging under-represented adults in career guidance and training is possible, but requires considerable time and financial investment, and a mobilisation of key community resources.

- Provincial and territorial governments should dedicate funding to actively reach out to vulnerable adults in their communities and workplaces and better target career guidance services to their needs.

References

Carpentieri, J. et al. (2018), *GOAL Guidance and Orientation for Adult Learning. Final cross-country evaluation report*, UCL Institute of Education, https://adultguidance.eu/images/Reports/GOAL_final_cross-country_evaluation_report.pdf.   [2]

Cedefop et al. (2020), *Career Guidance Policy and Practice in the Pandemic. Results of a Joint International Survey*, https://data.europa.eu/doi/10.2801/318103.   [1]

Joncas, J. and A. Pilote (2021), "The role of guidance professionals in enhancing the capabilities of marginalized students: the case of indigenous women in Canada", *International Journal for Educational and Vocational Guidance*, Vol. 21, pp. 405-427, http://dx.doi.org/10.1007/s10775-021-09474-3.   [3]

Michaud, G. et al. (2012), *Développement d'une approche visant à mobiliser la clientèle dite éloignée du marché du travail. Rapport final de la recherche déposé au ministère de l'Emploi et de la Solidarité sociale*, Université de Sherbrooke, http://bv.cdeacf.ca/EA_PDF/161000.pdf.   [4]

Note

[1] Labour and Immigration Ministry in collaboration with Community and Social Services, Advanced Education and Indigenous Relations.

3 Promoting high-quality career guidance service provision in Canada

This chapter reviews survey evidence on how satisfied adult users of career guidance in Canada are with the services they received, to what extent services were tailored to their needs, and which outcomes they report. It then discusses three key policy measures to strengthen the career guidance sector and service provision: producing and using high-quality labour market information; holding providers accountable and monitoring outcomes; and standardising the training and qualifications of career guidance advisors.

Summary

Survey evidence suggests that a large majority of adults in Canada (81%) are satisfied with the career guidance services they have received, which is comparable to the OECD average (79%). Compared with other OECD countries, adults in Canada were also more likely to indicate that career guidance services were useful to achieving reported employment and training outcomes. At the same time, there is room to better tailor career guidance in Canada to adults' needs. There are a few ways provincial and territorial governments can continue to strengthen the career guidance sector, and promote high-quality service provision.

First, reliable labour market information (LMI) is a key component of a high-performing career guidance system. The Labour Market Information Council (LMIC) together with the provinces and territories are working on making LMI more granular and accessible to citizens and career guidance advisors. Particular emphasis should be put on making LMI easy to access and understand, and training career guidance advisors in its use and interpretation.

Second, systems to hold government-funded providers accountable and monitoring the outcomes of services can be conducive to high-quality service provision. Provinces and territories have different systems in place, which typically involve public procurement processes and outcome-based funding. While an overly narrow focus on job placements might be detrimental to the quality of career guidance, clearly defined outcome indicators are useful to measure and evaluate the success of career guidance programmes. This is particularly valuable when integrated into a larger policy strategy or framework.

Third, standardising the training and qualifications of career guidance advisors will help to further strengthen career guidance provision across the country. In Canada, as in other OECD countries, career guidance advisors are not a regulated occupation, except in Quebec. A common requirement to work in the field, however, is a relevant tertiary qualification. Canada is a frontrunner with respect to the existing competency framework for career guidance advisors in Canada, the voluntary certifications available in five provinces, and the current development of a pan-Canadian certification standard. Government co-ordination on the implementation of a voluntary, pan-Canadian certification is an important step towards reducing mobility barriers for career guidance advisors and increasing the consistency of service provision. More could be done to offer continuing training for career guidance advisors who work in publicly-funded services and might not hold a certification.

This chapter reviews survey data on satisfaction with career guidance services and outcomes of career guidance reported by adult users in Canada. It then explores different policy measures to promote high-quality career guidance service provision, with reference to international best practice examples.

3.1. Satisfaction rates and reported outcomes of career guidance in Canada

Career guidance for adults has the potential to improve employment, education and training outcomes for individuals, while mitigating skills shortages and facilitating job transitions on labour markets. Empirical literature suggests that career guidance is effective at improving learning outcomes and training participation among adults, and there is some evidence on positive employment outcomes (Box 3.1. This section provides insights from the Survey of Career Guidance for Adults (SCGA) into the experiences adults have with career guidance in Canada as well as the outcomes they report as a result of the service. It then discusses to what extent career guidance services are tailored to adults' needs, citing existing approaches by different provinces to personalise services.

3.1.1. Satisfaction with career guidance is relatively high in Canada, and adults report a range of positive employment, education or training outcomes

Most adults in Canada are satisfied with the career guidance services they have received, though there is variation across provinces and between sub-groups. Eighty-one per cent of adult users of career guidance in Canada report being very satisfied or satisfied with the services, which is just above the OECD average of 79% (see Figure 3.1). The same share (81%) find guidance useful, while a lower percentage (67%) of adults find guidance well targeted. As elsewhere, there is room for making guidance more targeted to individuals' needs (Figure 3.3). Satisfaction rates with services were lower for older adults (72%) and for adults living in rural areas (73%) in Canada, suggesting more could be done to improve services for these groups.[1] Satisfaction rates were highest in Quebec (83%), Ontario (82%), and British Colombia (82%) and a bit lower in the Prairies (76%) and the Atlantic provinces (76%).

Figure 3.1. User satisfaction and perception of career guidance

Share of adults who used career services in the past five years, by reported satisfaction/perception

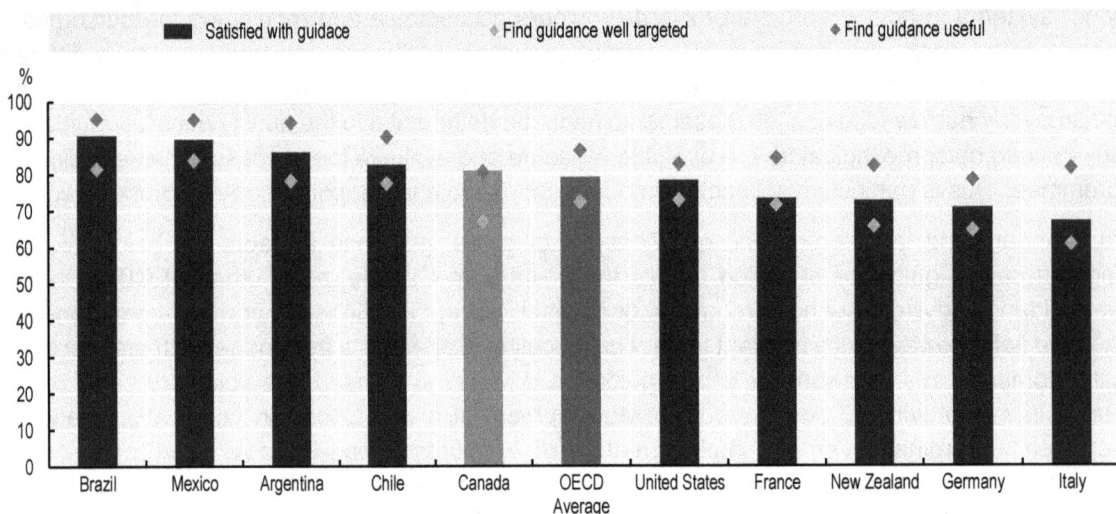

Note: The OECD Average includes Argentina, Brazil, Canada, Chile, France, Germany, Italy, Mexico, New Zealand and the United States. Data refer to the last time the respondent used career services (in the case of Canada) or spoke to a career guidance advisor (for all other countries). The categories reflect adults who are "very satisfied" or "satisfied" with guidance, find guidance "very well targeted" or "well targeted" and "very useful" or "useful". For details on the methodology, see Annex B.
Source: OECD 2020/2021 Survey of Career Guidance for Adults (SCGA).

Box 3.1. Evidence on the outcomes of career guidance for adults

Theoretical research has argued that career guidance brings many benefits for individuals, companies and governments. Career guidance for adults provides a link between education, training and the labour market, facilitates a better matching of labour market supply and demand and supports labour market participation of vulnerable groups. Through these pathways, it can positively impact economic productivity as well as social equity and inclusion. For companies, career guidance might help to increase productivity and reduce staff turnover. On an individual level, career guidance along the life-course may support adults' transitions into and within the labour market, increase their wages and job satisfaction (Percy and Dodd, 2021[1]; Barnes et al., 2020[2]).

Empirical evidence shows that career guidance can have a positive impact on short-term learning outcomes of individuals, such as decision-making skills, self-awareness or job search skills (Bimrose and Barnes, 2008[3]; Maguire, 2004[4]; Kidd, Jackson and Hirsh, 2003[5]; Hughes et al., 2002[6]). Career guidance has also been found to strengthen confidence and motivation (Bimrose and Barnes, 2008[3]), and improve adults' attitudes towards learning (European Commission, 2015[7]). For instance, an evaluation conducted in Ontario finds that a career guidance programme for adults in the automotive sector increased participants' sense of job-related self-efficacy (Reavley, 2013[8]).

Moreover, several impact evaluations have found a significant positive effect of career guidance on adults' participation in education or training (Lane et al., 2017[9]; Tyers and Sinclair, 2005[10]; Killeen and Kidd, 1991[11]). Some evidence also shows that career guidance improves employment outcomes, in particular supporting the job placement of unemployed adults as part of active labour market programmes (Liu, Huang and Wang, 2014[12]; Graversen and van Ours, 2008[13]; Hughes et al., 2002[6]). An impact evaluation from the United States finds that intensive employment services, including personalised career guidance and accompanying services, increased participants' earnings by 7 to 20 percent in the 30-month follow-up period (Fortson et al., 2017[14])

Figure 3.2. Employment, education and training outcomes of career guidance, Canada

Share of adults in Canada who used career services in the past five years, by reported outcome

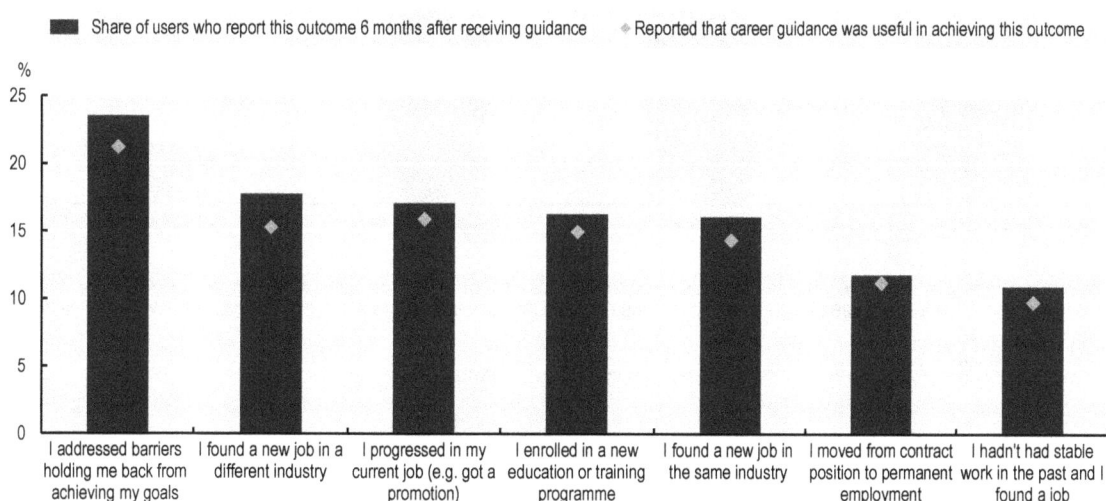

Note: Respondents could choose more than one answer. Data refers to the last time the respondent used career services. Respondents were asked whether any of these outcomes occurred within six months of receiving career guidance.
Source: OECD 2020/2021 Survey of Career Guidance for Adults (SCGA).

Nearly all users (99%) of career guidance in Canada reported at least one positive outcome related to employment, education or training six months after receiving a career guidance service (Figure 3.2). Almost a quarter (24%) of users reported that they addressed barriers that held them back from achieving their goals within half a year after receiving guidance. These goals included improved health, stable housing, stronger support network or greater clarity about what they want. In Canada, career guidance seems to support professional development, with a share of adults saying that they progressed in their current job (17%), or found a new job in the same industry (16%) after using the service. Sixteen per cent (16%) of adults who received career guidance services also reported to have enrolled in a new education or training programme afterwards. Compared to other OECD countries, adults in Canada were more likely to indicate that the career guidance services they received were useful to achieve the reported employment, education or training outcomes they experienced (Figure 3.2).

3.1.2. There is room to better tailor career guidance services in Canada to adults' needs

While high satisfaction rates and good outcomes from users indicate a relatively high quality of career guidance services in Canada, there is room to better tailor services to adults' needs. According to the SCGA, 67% of adults in Canada who have used career guidance services reported that services were very targeted or targeted to their personal needs. While this represents the majority of career guidance users, it falls below the OECD average of 73% (Figure 3.3).

Figure 3.3. Tailoring career guidance services to individual needs

Share of adults who used career services the past five years, by degree to which they reported that the service targeted their individual needs

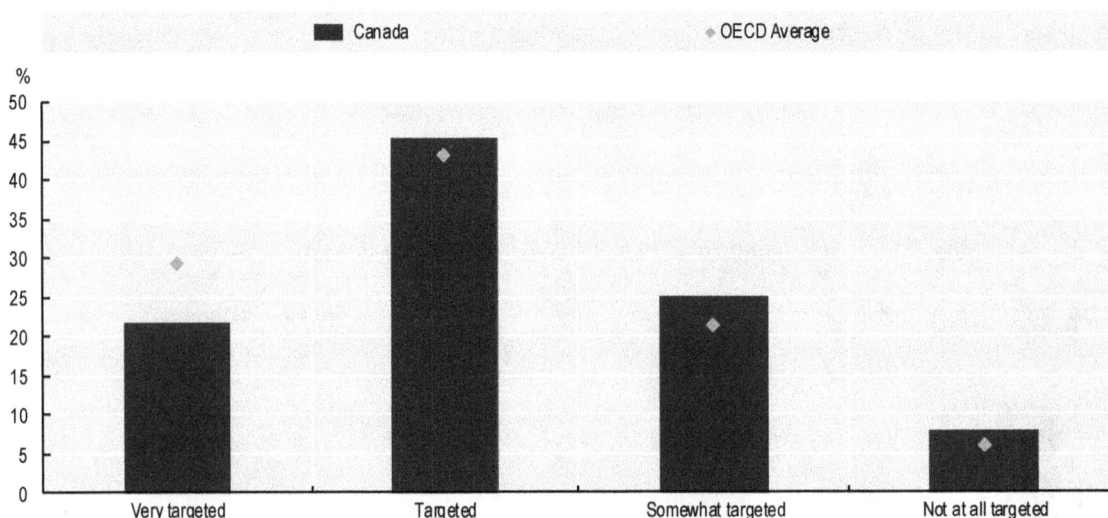

Note: The OECD average includes Argentina, Brazil, Canada, Chile, France, Germany, Italy, Mexico, New Zealand and the United States. Data refer to the last time the respondent used a career service (in the case of Canada) or spoke to a career guidance advisor (in the case of other countries in the survey).
Source: OECD 2020/2021 Survey of Career Guidance for Adults (SCGA).

Tailoring career guidance services to adults' needs requires taking the time to understand clients' objectives and to assess their unique skills. Skills assessments, the recognition of prior learning, and individual career development roadmaps can be useful tools in doing so. If services are narrowly focused on matching jobseekers quickly with jobs, without considering the persistent and intersecting barriers adults experience in finding sustainable, high-quality employment, they can create a negative cycle in which adults rotate back and forth between periods of employment in poorly fitting jobs and periods of unemployment.

Career guidance services in the provinces apply different types of skills assessments. Most commonly, adults who used career guidance services in Canada reported that they were interviewed about their skills and experience (69%). Twenty-nine per cent of career guidance users had their skills assessed through one or several tests, 19% were asked about performance evaluations from work, and 18% about their qualifications or certificates (see Figure 3.4). In Quebec, for instance, employment service providers conduct an initial skills assessment interview, which takes into account the profile and specific needs of individuals. This can lead to a recognition of prior learning (*reconnaissance des acquis et des compétences, RAC*) process that allows to offer targeted support for adults. For immigrants or refugees, the government of Ontario offers a Coordinated Language Assessment and Referral System (CLARS), which assesses their language skills through a network of language assessment centres that can be an entry point for further education and training.

Figure 3.4. Skills assessment as part of career guidance services

Share of adults in Canada reporting that their skills have been assessed by the career practitioner, by type of assessment

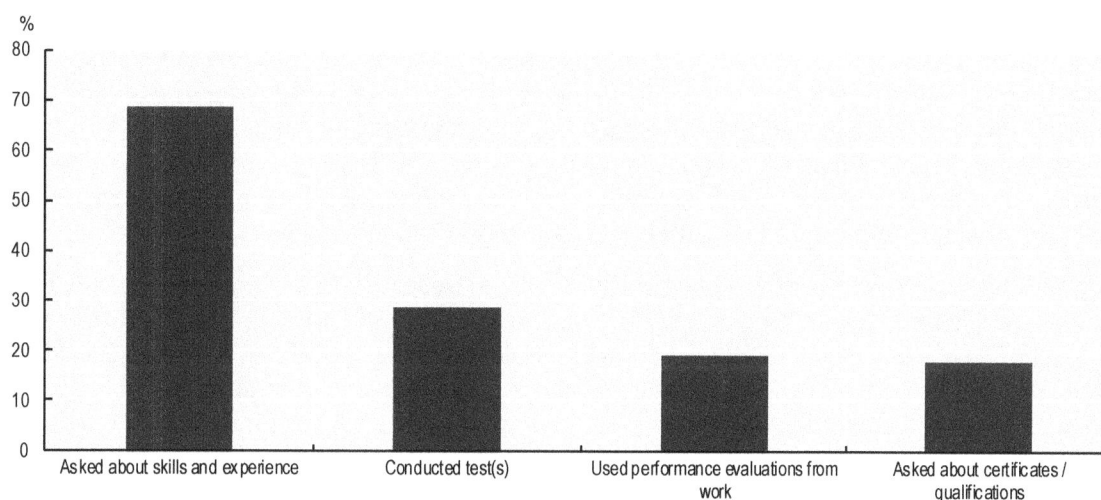

Note: Data refer to respondents who have used a career service in the last 5 years, and to the last time they did so.
Source: OECD 2020/2021 Survey of Career Guidance for Adults (SCGA).

The particular tools career guidance advisors apply to assess adults' skills and competences vary across service providers and province or territory. Some service providers in Canada have adopted the PRIME Employability Dimensions framework (Box 3.7). They use PRIME as the basis for the initial assessment of adults' skills and employment readiness when the adult first enters career guidance services, and subsequently measure progressive change along these employability dimensions during and after the adult has received the service. ESDC's Skills for Success model is another conceptual framework used to measure adults' skills. On their website, ESDC provides a range of tools for individuals to assess and develop their skills (ESDC, 2021[15]).

Following assessment, the recognition of prior learning is a more formal type of skills validation, which can be an important part of career guidance services. It can help to make the skills adults already have visible, especially if they were acquired through non-formal learning on the job, or as part of a foreign qualification by immigrants or refugees. Formally recognising the skills and competences adults have shortens their upskilling pathways, thus accelerating transitions to new jobs or sectors. The government of Ontario, for example, requires school boards to provide a Prior Learning Assessment and Recognition (PLAR) process to mature students who seek to complete high school education. This is mandated by a specific policy memorandum and includes an individualised assessment of adults' skills, experience and prior learning or education as part of a formal evaluation process. Adults may obtain credits for prior learning that count towards their diploma (Government of Ontario, 2003[16]). In Quebec, a network of services called SARCA (*services d'accueil, de référence, de conseil et d'accompagnement*) is offered in adult education centres and vocational training centres. SARCA provides career guidance and career information to adults, and accompanies them in a recognition of prior learning process (*reconnaissance des acquis et des compétences, RAC*) to obtain a secondary school or a vocational diploma. Some OECD countries have established systems for the recognition of prior learning that are linked with career guidance. In Portugal, for instance, more than 300 *Qualifica* centres across the country combine career guidance services with the recognition of prior learning, primarily targeting adults with low qualifications, the unemployed and young people.

Personalised career development roadmaps are individual action or training plans that adults co-develop with career guidance advisors. They have shown to be powerful tools that can motivate adults to take action towards reaching their employment and learning goals. According to the SCGA, 59% of adult users of career guidance in Canada receive such a personalised career development roadmap, which is above the OECD average of 55%. In Ontario, the Creating Pathways to Success Programme encourages the use of an online Individual Pathways Plan for secondary students, including adult learners. Other services with a career guidance component in Ontario also have a focus on developing an individualised career or learning pathway: the Bridge Training programme for skilled immigrants and refugees, the Literacy and Basic skills programme, and employment services. Use of personalised career development roadmaps is highest in Ontario and Quebec and lowest in the Atlantic provinces (Figure 3.5), suggesting room for improvement in this region.

Figure 3.5. Personalised career development roadmaps as part of career guidance services

Share of adults who report receiving a personalised career development roadmap as part of career guidance services, by country and region

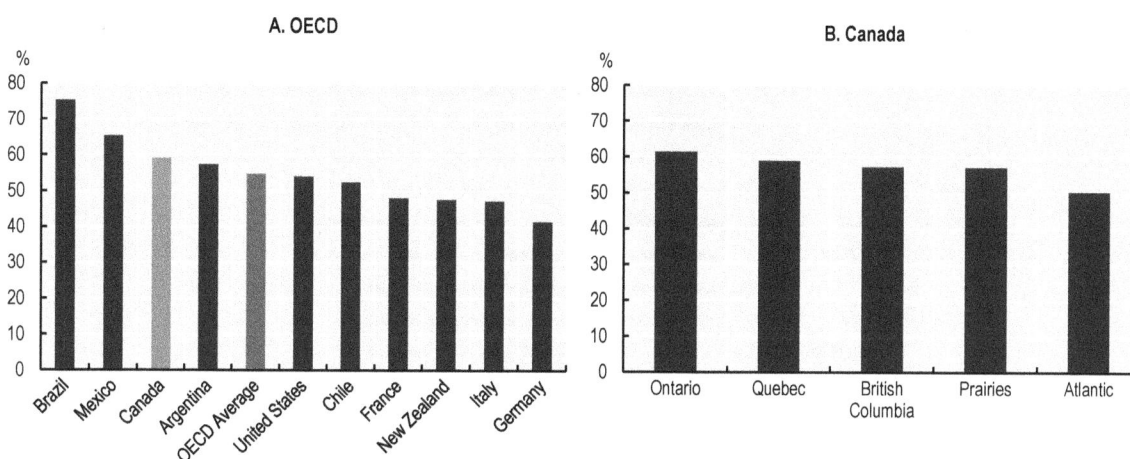

Notes: The OECD Average includes Argentina, Brazil, Canada, Chile, France, Germany, Italy, Mexico, New Zealand and the United States. Data refer to the last time the respondent spoke to a career guidance advisor. In Canada, data refer to the last time the adults used career services. The Atlantic region includes Newfoundland and Labrador, Prince Edward Island, Nova Scotia and New Brunswick. The Prairie region includes Manitoba, Saskatchewan and Alberta. Sample sizes in the territories were too low to be included.
Source: OECD 2020/2021 Survey of Career Guidance for Adults (SCGA).

The findings of the SCGA, as well as stakeholder interviews suggest that existing services in Canada are of high-quality, and strategic policy can help to maintain this performance and bring about greater consistency in service provision across provinces and territories. Responses from policy questionnaires sent out for this project suggest that there is room to improve consistency in career guidance service delivery within and across provinces and territories. Findings from the SCGA confirm these regional differences in the use of career guidance among adults in Canada, both across and within provinces. The following sections describe three key policy measures to strengthen the career guidance system in Canada and promote high-quality and consistent service provision: producing and using high-quality labour market information, holding providers accountable and monitoring outcomes and standardising training and qualifications of career guidance advisors.

3.2. Producing and using high-quality labour market information

An important component of effective career guidance is labour market information (LMI) that is objective, timely, sufficiently granular, fit-for-purpose, and well-co-ordinated (OECD, 2016[17]). High-quality LMI is important for career guidance advisors to provide their clients with accurate advice on current and future labour markets. On an aggregate level, good LMI can help to promote the development of skills which are in high demand on the labour market, by motivating adults to invest in those skills.

Those adults in Canada who participate in career guidance services receive much of the information they are looking for, with some exceptions (Figure 3.6). According to the SCGA, users most often receive information on skills requirements (37% of users), job vacancies (35%), wages (26%), and projected future job openings (22%). By contrast, the type of LMI which adults in Canada most frequently demand is information on wages (40% of adults), job vacancies (39%) as well as skills and education requirement of jobs (38% and 27%, respectively). Figure 3.6 suggests that adults would like to receive certain types of information more than they currently do: salaries and wages, financial support, and certification and education requirements.

Figure 3.6. Type of information sought and received during career guidance, Canada

Share of adults who used career services in the past five years, by type of information they received; and share of adults by type of information they will seek the next time they use career information or guidance services

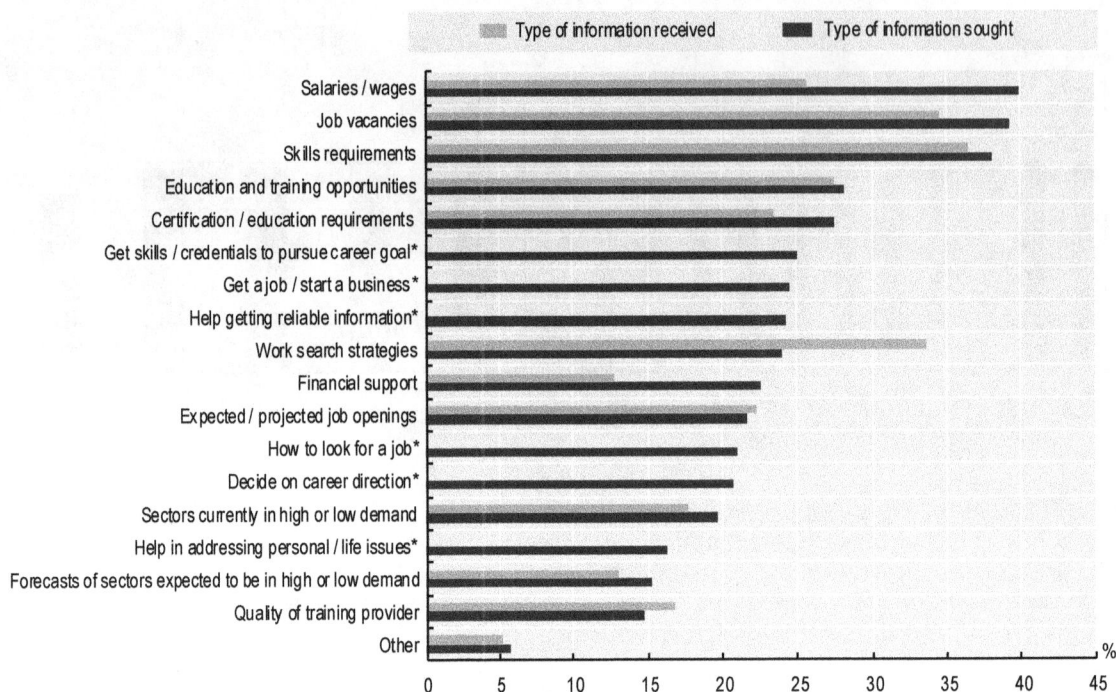

Note: Respondents could choose more than one answer. Data refers to the last time the respondent used career services. Some answer responses were not available for the question on 'type of information' received, and are marked with an asterisk.
Source: OECD 2020/2021 Survey of Career Guidance for Adults (SCGA).

In Canada, the responsibility for the production and dissemination of LMI is shared among the different levels of government. As part of these responsibilities, the federal, provincial and territorial governments have created and funded since 2017 the Labour Market Information Council (LMIC) to improve the reliability and availability of LMI, and to close gaps in the data collection, analysis and dissemination of skills-related data (LMIC, 2021[18]). The LMIC is a pan-Canadian not-for-profit led by a Board of Directors composed of senior government officials from federal, provincial and territorial governments and Statistics Canada. According to its first strategic plan, LMIC focuses on developing local, granular data, a better understanding of current and future skill demands as well as the disseminating LMI for a diversity of users (LMIC, 2018[19]).

Besides making high-quality LMI available, career guidance advisors also need to feel comfortable using it. A workshop with career guidance advisors hosted by LMIC showed that a key challenge is advisors' limited time and ability to extract meaningful insights from technical or lengthy reports. This underscores the need for tools and resources that are easy to use, free to access, and conducive to help practitioners to navigate LMI (LMIC, 2021[20]).

One way to make better use of LMI is to train career guidance advisors in locating and interpreting it. A recent LMIC survey found that only three out of five practitioners surveyed (60%) think labour market information is easy to understand, and fewer than half (43%) say they have received training to help them access or make sense of the data (LMIC, 2019[21]). Several OECD countries have programmes to train career guidance advisors in using LMI, including the *Cités des Métiers* centres in Belgium. Their staff participate in weekly LMI sessions delivered by an expert. In France, career guidance advisors working for the Conseil en Évolution Professionnelle (CEP), a network of service providers dedicated to career guidance for employed adults, receive training sessions to stay up-to-date about government reforms, economic changes, labour market cycles, innovations and digital transformations affecting the labour market.

3.2.1. Labour market information is disseminated through online portals across Canada

Online portals are a common way to make LMI available for individuals and career guidance advisors across Canada. The Canadian Job Bank (Box 3.2) is an example of an accessible platform that aggregates online job vacancies from across Canada in a single platform. This is rare in international comparison. In addition to this federal-level online portal, each of the provinces and the Northwest Territories maintain their own online portals. Most of these feature regional LMI, and some also have information particularly for disadvantaged groups (see Table 3.1). Few, however, offer skills assessments or skills gap analysis, which would allow an adult to identify the skills, certificates or qualifications they would need to pursue a given occupation. Box 3.3 shares examples of an online career guidance portal used in France that exploits artificial intelligence to provide tailored employment and training suggestions for adults based on existing LMI.

Box 3.2. Job Bank as a federal-level online portal

Job Bank is a job search tool and online employment resource run by Employment and Social Development Canada (ESDC) in collaboration with the provincial and territorial governments. It provides a free platform across Canada that connects individuals looking for employment with firms that want to hire. Approximately 5 million users visit the website every month.

A variety of LMI and tools are made available by Job Bank. Users can browse job postings by region, and set up job alerts. Career guidance resources and labour market information can be searched by region, sector, occupation, wages and by economic outlook. Companies, in turn, can access information about how to recruit, manage and train employees. Job Bank also provides a range of self-assessment tools, such as personality, interests and skills tests. Some are specifically targeted to Indigenous people, persons with disabilities, visible minorities, young people and veterans.

Job Bank is designed to support employment insurance policies and labour market objectives. As such, it has played an important role during the pandemic, both with respect to connecting laid off workers to vacant positions, and as a resource to inform them about available emergency benefit schemes. The website is an accessible, secure and unified platform used across Canada.

An evaluation found that between 2018 and 2019, over 1.2 million job opportunities were posted on Job Bank. Low-educated individuals (i.e. those with a high school degree or less) were overrepresented among users, while the age of users corresponded roughly to the age distribution of the Canadian labour market. The evaluation concluded that a majority of job seekers (60%) were satisfied with the job matching service of Job Board; however, employers and partners were more critical about its value-added, citing poor quality of job matches as a reason (Government of Canada, 2021[22]).

Source: Government of Canada (2021[23]), Job Bank, https://www.jobbank.gc.ca/home; Government of Canada (2021[22]), *Evaluation of the Job Match Service connecting Job Seekers to Canadian Employers. Final Report.*, https://www.canada.ca/content/dam/esdc-edsc/documents/corporate/reports/evaluations/job-match-connecting-job-seekers-employers/jobMatchReport-en.pdf; OECD 2021 Policy Questionnaire 'Career Guidance for Adults in Canada', Employment and Social Development Canada (ESDC).

Table 3.1. Online portals developed by the provinces and territories

Province	Name of website	Web address	LMI	Skills assessment	Job search advice	Job board	Information for disadvantaged groups
Alberta	Alis Alberta	https://alis.alberta.ca	x	x	x	x	x
British Columbia	WorkBC	https://www.workbc.ca/	x		x	x	x
Manitoba	Manitoba Career Development	http://www.manitobacareerdevelopment.ca/			x		x
	Manitoba Career Prospects	https://manitobacareerprospects.ca/					x
New Brunswick	NBJobs	https://www.nbjobs.ca/	x			x	x
Newfoundland and Labrador	Immigration, Population Growth and Skills	https://www.gov.nl.ca/ipgs/employ-support/for-individuals/				x	x
		https://www.gov.nl.ca/labourmarketinformation	x				
Northwest Territories	Career, Employment and Training Services	https://www.ece.gov.nt.ca/en/services/career-and-employment	x				
Nova Scotia	Explore Careers	https://explorecareers.novascotia.ca/	x				
		https://novascotiaworks.ca/nsdc	x		x	x	
Ontario	Choose a career	https://www.ontario.ca/page/choose-career	x				
Prince Edward Island	Career Development Services	https://cdspei.ca/			x	x	
Quebec	Emploi-Québec	https://www.quebec.ca/emploi/	x		x	x	
	Emplois d'Avenir	https://www.emploisdavenir.gouv.qc.ca/	x				
Saskatchewan	SaskJobs – Career Services	https://www.saskatchewan.ca/residents/jobs-working-and-training/saskjobs-career-services	x			x	

Source: Author's own compilation.

Box 3.3. Using innovative technology in career guidance services

Bob is an online career guidance tool used by the **French** public employment service, *Pole Emploi*. It leverages artificial intelligence (AI) to support people navigate their job search. Bob provides a tailored action plan and coaching, which aims to help adults overcome their barriers to employment. Users are asked to answer questions about their career aspirations, expected wage, experience or education level. On this basis, the tool proposes next steps users may want to take in order to reach their goals, for instance, to participate in training. Suggestions are based on different sources of data, including existing job classifications, vacancy data, data on job seeker pathways and employment outcomes.

SkillLab, a startup software company based in the **Netherlands**, has developed a mobile application that uses artificial intelligence to help individuals identify their skills, explore careers and apply for jobs. In particular, it allows a granular skills assessment that aims to capture adults' prior learning and employment experience and identifies skill gaps as well as relevant local training and employment opportunities. The application is available in different languages and particularly targeted at disadvantaged job seekers, such as refugees and migrants. It is designed to support career guidance advisors to personalise their services and better support their clients. The benefit of AI applications is that they are easily scalable and able to provide tailored suggestions for adults based on existing labour market information.

CareerLabsVR is a career guidance tool developed with support of the government of **Ontario** under the lead of the Employment and Education Centre, a partner of Employment Ontario. It allows young people and job seekers to explore career pathways through virtual reality (VR). Users can run simulations where they experience different professional roles in an interactive 3D environment. The initial simulation modules are designed to promote learning about in-demand careers in the steel and aluminium industries, for instance, including robotics technicians, process engineers, or construction welders. Further modules are developed for skilled trades and agricultural jobs. In the future, the virtual reality modules can be used by employment service providers across the province.

Source: Verhagen (2021[24]), Opportunities and challenges of using AI for training, https://doi.org/10.1787/22729bd6-en; https://www.bob-emploi.fr/; https://skilllab.io/en-us; https://careerlabsvr.com/.

3.3. Holding providers accountable and monitoring outcomes

Governments have an interest in holding providers of publicly-funded career guidance accountable and monitoring the outcomes of services, to ensure high-quality services for citizens. Especially when contracting third-party service providers, governments want to ensure that funding is used for effective services that are in line with larger policy targets. Contracting out employment services, including career guidance offers many potential benefits: increased flexibility to scale capacity according to need, cost-effectiveness, and a better tailoring of services through specialised service providers (Langenbucher and Vodopivec, 2022[25]). Achieving these benefits depends on the actual design and monitoring of the contracting arrangements that are put in place. The following section discusses two mechanisms that most provincial governments in Canada have in place to manage third-party provision of career guidance that is delivered as part of government-funded employment services: public procurement and outcome-based funding.

3.3.1. Provinces have public procurement processes to ensure the quality of career guidance

A common mechanism by the provinces to hold third-party providers of career guidance to account are public procurement processes. Contracted services often follow an application-based public tender, with an open call for proposals by third-party providers that are in line with particular policy objectives and programme requirements. Contracts spell out certain target outcomes and determine the type of reporting or monitoring mechanisms in place for a specified period of time, usually between 1 and 3 years. If third-party providers do not meet the target outcomes or their contractual responsibilities, they might not be selected in the next cycle of public procurement. In Nova Scotia, for instance, qualified organisations can apply to the NS Employment Assistance Program through a call for proposals. This programme sets out the specific requirements for service delivery, such as regular reporting on targets and activities, and the adherence to certain service standards. In Alberta, the accountability mechanism with third-party providers is particularly comprehensive, specifying clear roles and responsibilities (Box 3.4). Outcome-based contract management is also applied in Saskatchewan and Ontario.

Box 3.4. Procurement of career guidance service providers in Alberta

The Government of Alberta offers career guidance services through employment and training programmes delivered by contracted third-party providers. The Government posts a public request for proposals online. In the case of Workforce Partnership programs, which are set up in response to consultations with key stakeholders, the procurement process allows the Government of Alberta to react rather flexibly to a pressing labour market need.

If successful in the competition, service providers provide the defined service over a specified time period according to the terms and conditions specified in the contract. The Income and Employment Supports Policy Manual provides a framework of accountability and quality, determining the roles and responsibilities for external service providers in Alberta. If providers do not deliver the desired quality of service, their chances to be selected in the next round of public procurement are lower.

To measure the performance of service providers after the procurement process, the Government of Alberta conducts periodic evaluations, measuring the entry into employment or education and training by individuals who participated in the respective programme. Other indicators that are monitored include participation, completion and satisfaction of adults in the programmes.

Source: OECD 2021 Policy Questionnaire 'Career Guidance for Adults in Canada'; Government of Alberta (2021[26]), *Income and Employment Supports Policy Manual*, http://www.humanservices.alberta.ca/AWOnline/3813.html (accessed 16 September 2021).

While procurement processes and outcome-based contract management are valuable to ensure the accountability and quality of third-party service providers, their design matters. Unintentionally, these mechanisms can establish a culture of competition rather than collaboration and impose a significant administrative burden on third-party service providers. If resources of third-party providers are overly limited as a result, this may ultimately be to the detriment of service quality, and contribute to organisational instability and high staff turnover. A recent OECD working paper highlights the need to carefully consider questions related to the design and implementation of outcome-based contract management: fostering competition amongst potential providers, setting appropriate minimum service requirements and prices for different client groups, and ensuring the accountability of providers through monitoring and evaluations (Langenbucher and Vodopivec, 2022[25]). Procurement and accountability mechanisms for third-party providers can be very positive interventions if they are linked to appropriate outcome measures that do not put an overly limited focus on rapid, and potentially temporary job placements.

Two in five OECD countries partially or fully subcontract public employment services, often including career guidance, to third-party providers. Examples from Australia and Belgium illustrate innovative design features that are possible for contracted employment and career guidance services (Box 3.5).

Box 3.5. Third-party provision of employment and career guidance services in the OECD

Outsourcing career guidance through vouchers in Flanders (Belgium)

The public employment services of the Belgian region of Flanders, called *Vlaamse Dienst voor Arbeidsbemiddeling en Beroepsopleiding* (VDAB) has been outsourcing intensive coaching and mediation services for jobseekers, and issuing career guidance vouchers to employed individuals. Public procurement is linked to quality requirements and minimal service descriptions. Individuals have the right of up to two vouchers every six years, and each voucher offers four hours of subsidised career guidance. Clients can choose the provider they prefer. While the satisfaction rate with services is very high, one concern is that the vouchers do not reach vulnerable groups such as low-skilled workers.

The New Employment Services Trial in Australia

Australia has piloted a new model of service provision in Adelaide South in South Australia and the Mid North Coast in New South Wales between 2019 and 2021. The New Employment Services Trial (NEST) is in preparation to be launched mid-2022 across the country. Key aspects of the new service model are a focus on digital services on a comprehensive online platform, a payment model that considers the intensity of barriers to employment clients face when reimbursing third-party providers, as well as a new IT system.

Source: Langenbucher and Vodopivec (2022[25]), Paying for results: Contracting out employment services through outcome-based payment schemes in OECD countries, https://dx.doi.org/10.1787/c6392a59-en; Department of Education Skills and Employment (2021[27]), "NESA National Conference: The New Employment Services Trial and the OES the DESE and Provider Experience", https://www.dese.gov.au/collections/new-employment-service-trial-nest-guidelines (accessed 23 January 2022).

In some OECD countries, providers are only eligible to provide publicly-funded career guidance if they hold a given certification or meet certain quality standards (OECD, 2021[28]). The benefit of these approaches is an additional layer of quality assurance, often guaranteed by external review. In Austria, for example, providers of the country's free career guidance programme must be certified by the special IBOBB (Information, Counselling and Orientation for Education and Career) certification. In France, career guidance advisors who participate in the national career guidance programme (*Conseil en evolution professionnelle, CEP*) have to conform to quality requirements (*cahier de charges*), which specify objectives, beneficiary groups, service provision, methods, and the skill requirements of advisors. In Korea, service providers that carry out the Employment Success Package Programme (ESPP) need to pass a comprehensive yearly performance evaluation by the government in order to participate in the programme the following year.

3.3.2. Monitoring the outcomes of career guidance services is increasingly linked to funding

Responses to the OECD 2021 Policy Questionnaire 'Career Guidance for Adults in Canada' indicate a general trend towards outcome-based funding. While many provinces specify target outcomes in contracts with third-party providers of career guidance services, only some directly link outcome measurements to funding. For some programmes in British Columbia, funding is directly tied to performance. That is, service providers receive payments when they meet certain predefined outcomes. In British Colombia's Skills Training for Employment programme targeted at vulnerable and underrepresented populations, payments are made on a per-participant basis at various progress markers (project initiation, completion, employment, and sustained employment).

In principle, outcome-based funding can have a strong steering function to incentivise high-quality services; however, attention needs to be paid to which particular indicators are tied to funding. Incentives to reduce time spent with individual clients and quickly place them into jobs might be unsustainable and more costly in the long run. For the most part, outcome-based funding is tied to hard outcomes, such as employment status, income levels or participation in education and training. Though harder to measure, tying funding to more subjective soft outcomes of career guidance - such as health and well-being, self-efficacy, social integration, or attitudinal changes - is a promising way to incentivise high-quality services.

One way to use funding to incentivise high-quality services is to provide extra funding as a reward for excellent performance. This is implemented in Nova Scotia, where a performance-related top-up of the base funding encourages third-party providers to improve and innovate their services (Box 3.6).

Box 3.6. Performance-related funding for employment services in Nova Scotia

In Nova Scotia, all adults can access employment assistance services, which include career guidance. These services are delivered by a network of third-party service providers under a common brand called Nova Scotia Works, which consists of 16 community-based employment service providers across the province. At the base of this service system is the Nova Scotia Works Accountability Framework, which is part of an ongoing policy process for strategic planning and outcome monitoring.

Service providers that are associated with the Nova Scotia Works network receive top-up performance achievement funding when their clients achieve outcome targets towards sustained labour force attachment. Key performance indicators are monitored and if certain outcomes are met, this results in additional funding to reward the achievement of certain outcomes. These indicators include, for example, the job placement of underrepresented clients, or sustained labour force attachment (employed after 24 weeks, employed after 52 weeks). Providers receive these payments as an additional grant to the base funding that covers programme and administrative costs. All payments are per-client / per-outcome payments.

The performance-related revenue allows employment service providers to fund activities outside of direct service provision, for instance, community capacity building, and investment in project innovation or quality improvement.

Source: OECD 2021 Policy Questionnaire 'Career Guidance for Adults in Canada'; Employment Nova Scotia (2019[29]), Nova Scotia Works Accountability Framework Strategic Plan; Employment Nova Scotia (2021[30]), Nova Scotia Employment Assistance Services Policy.

While some provinces and service providers only collect minimum information on the outcomes of career guidance services, others employ a more sophisticated range of indicators and measurement tools. Standard indicators are the participation and completion rates of programmes, as well as the employment outcomes of adults after having participated in a programme. To support transparent contracting of third-party service providers, for instance, Saskatchewan has adopted the PRIME tool for skills and employability assessment, reporting and analysis (Box 3.7), and Newfoundland and Labrador, in collaboration with community partners, is in the process of doing so. In Alberta, career and employment services that are funded under the Career and Employment Information Services (CEIS) Grant have an internal dashboard of key performance indicators (KPIs). These are used to monitor service provision and client outcomes and are updated quarterly. KPIs include, for instance, the total number of clients who participated in CEIS (overall and by service type), the share of former

CEIS clients who found employment after participation, and the average and median monthly incomes of former CEIS client who found employment after participating in CEIS.

As outcomes of services are already measured in many parts of Canada, there is potential to establish a better evidence base through evaluations. Rather than using outcome measurements as a mere reporting tool, they can be used to establish a rich evidence base about the impact of career guidance. Evaluations help identify good practice as well as areas for improvement in the system of career guidance service delivery. Where career guidance is offered as part of more general employment services, it might be hard to single out its impact. Experiences from other OECD countries show that external bodies can provide unbiased monitoring and a systematic evaluation of services, including quality audits of providers and impact evaluations of career guidance programmes (OECD, 2021[28]). A prior OECD study recommended that the Future Skills Centre could establish quality standards to improve the impact evaluation culture in Canada (2020[31]).

Box 3.7. The PRIME Employability Assessment Tool

The Performance Recording Instrument for Meaningful Evaluation (PRIME) is an employability assessment tool used to assess individuals' employability strengths and needs and to measure the effect of services. It was developed by the Canadian Career Development Foundation (CCDF) in co-operation with provincial career guidance service providers. PRIME functions as a data management software that allows to track, report and analyse participant data and outcomes. It has been adopted to support service provision and an evaluation of the impact of career guidance in Saskatchewan.

PRIME allows career guidance advisors to collect data on employment and training outcomes, but also the quality of job matches and incremental progress towards employability. PRIME uses an Employability Dimensions Framework which maps broad categories of adults' needs and strengths, for instance, practical barriers to employment or indicators around skills needs. By measuring progress along a continuum, rather than only focusing on whether or not someone became employed or entered a training programme, it capture a richer picture of the impact of career guidance services.

What sets PRIME apart from other outcome measurement systems is that it not only provides meaningful insights for the funders of career guidance services, but is also designed to be a user-friendly tool that is used on a daily basis by practitioners to inform their practice, as well as for the clients themselves to see the progress they have made.

Source: OECD stakeholder interviews.

3.4. Standardising training and qualifications of career guidance advisors

The training and qualifications of career guidance advisors are perhaps the most essential ingredient to high-quality services. The following section discusses the requirements and regulations Canadian provinces and territories have in place for the practice of career guidance. It compares them to other OECD countries and deliberates on possible steps towards greater professionalisation, including a federal-level certification for career guidance advisors, called Career Development Practitioners (CDPs) in Canada.

3.4.1. Career guidance advisors are not a legally regulated occupation in Canada, except in Quebec

Career guidance advisors in Canada are generally required to hold tertiary qualifications in a related field, including psychology, education or social sciences, but do not need specialised education or training in career guidance. A 2019 CERIC survey of 1 350 career guidance advisors across Canada found that 41% held a Bachelor's degree, 35% a Master's degree and 18% a College certificate or diploma (CERIC, 2019[32]). In Quebec, guidance counsellors belong to a regulated occupational group and are required to hold a specialised diploma and a license to practice (Box 3.8).

There are exceptions in Canada where employers require career guidance advisors to have certain minimum level education, or a specific type of education or training. Usually, this depends on the specific service provider, or professional role in question. For instance, secondary school guidance counsellors in Ontario require specific advanced qualifications and must take part in ongoing professional development. In New Brunswick, the minimum level of education for a career guidance role is high school graduation plus 6 years of relevant work experience; however, the majority of applicants hold a Bachelor's degree. In British Columbia, each government-funded programme has its own set of criteria for funding, which can include requirements for career guidance advisors' training and qualification. The Government of Alberta does not require career practitioners to be certified to work within government services, but some employers prefer to hire certified career development practitioners.

Five provinces offer a voluntary professional certification (Alberta, British Columbia, New Brunswick, Nova Scotia, and Ontario) for career guidance advisors. Practitioners can acquire the certification through a recognition of prior learning procedure, and are then allowed to carry the title of Certified Career Development Practitioner (CCDP) (for further detail, see Table 3.2).

There is a separate process of certification for *career counsellors*, which is a related but distinct profession from career development practitioners (CDPs) in Canada. The approach that career counsellors take might be considered more therapeutic, with a particular consideration of mental health issues. While there is overlap in the roles of career development practitioners and career counsellors, the scope of practice, the required competencies and road to certification are distinct. The following sections focus on certification for career development practitioners, who "help individuals navigate learning and employment transitions across the lifespan" (Canadian Career Development Foundation and Canadian Council for Career Development, 2021[33]).

Quebec's hybrid model is an outlier in the regulatory landscape for career guidance advisors in Canada. Guidance counsellors, called *conseillers et conseillères d'orientation*, are a legally regulated professional group subject to specific occupational entry requirements (Box 3.8). While their areas of practice are similar to career counsellors in the rest of Canada, guidance counsellors play an important role in public service provision in Quebec, where the practice of all career guidance-related activities are reserved for them. All other career guidance advisors, including employment counsellors (*conseillers et conseillères en emploi*), are not subject to regulation in Quebec.

Box 3.8. The hybrid model of occupational regulation of career guidance in Quebec

In Quebec, guidance counsellors (*conseillers et conseillères d'orientation, C.O.*) are a professional group with a history of regulation through the occupational code of Quebec. The regulatory body is the *Ordre des conseillers et conseillères d'orientation du Québec (OCCOQ)*. OCCOQ sets entry requirements and also monitors the practice of its members according to the duties, obligations, values and ethics the law foresees for the occupation. In contrast to the other provinces, guidance counsellors are regulated by the occupational code of Quebec. In 2021, the OCCOQ had 2 619 members, of whom 48% worked in the educational sector, 16% in employment services and 14% in private consultancies.

Graduates with a relevant Master's degree in guidance counselling, career counselling, counselling psychology or *sciences de l'orientation* are automatically admitted to the profession, while those with a different educational background are subject to an application for admission by equivalence. Once admitted, members of the OCCOQ receive a licence that entitles them to carry the occupational title of C.O., and to exercise activities that are restricted to the profession. Their core services consist of counselling, guidance and career development for people of all ages and backgrounds, in particular for clients with mental or neuropsychological disorders, and physical or cognitive disabilities. In this respect, they are similar to *career counsellors* in the rest of Canada.

In Quebec, C.O.s are considered a separate occupational group from career guidance advisors who offer more general employment and career development services. Employment counsellors (*conseillers et conseillères en emploi*) and other career guidance advisors are not subject to an occupational license and can have a variety of degrees and educational backgrounds. While these professional groups do not currently have access to a certification, the recently founded *Association Québécoise des Professionnels du Développement de Carrière* (Quebec Association of Career Development Professionals) aims to increase their recognition.

Source: OCCOQ (2021[34]), Ordre des conseillers et conseillères d'orientation du Québec, https://www.orientation.qc.ca/ (accessed 5 August 2021); OCCOQ (2021[35]), Rapport Annuel 2020/2021, https://www.orientation.qc.ca/medias/iw/Rapport-annuel-OCCOQ-2020-2021.pdf (accessed 22 September 2021); https://www.aqpddc.com/ (accessed 18 October 2021).

> ### Box 3.9. The federal-level Competency Profile for Career Development Practitioners
>
> The Canadian Standards and Guidelines for Career Development Practitioners (S&Gs) were launched in 2001, following a comprehensive process of stakeholder consultation, and have been updated several times since. The federal government, through Human Resources Development Canada, funded their development as a voluntary competence framework in the field of career guidance. Being the first country to introduce such a framework, the Canadian S&Gs also formed the basis of an international competency framework by the International Association for Educational and Vocational Guidance (IAEVG).
>
> The S&Gs have been a widely used competence framework that has underpinned most career guidance training programmes as well as the available provincial certifications across Canada, with the exception of Quebec. In Nova Scotia, for instance, the S&Gs are the foundation of what is known as the 'Nova Scotia Profile', the competency profile against which individuals are assessed for certification. Beyond training and certifications, some employers in certain fields use the S&Gs for job postings and the identification of training needs.
>
> Respondents to the OECD policy questionnaire reported that the S&Gs have been inconsistently applied across organisations, and that there is scope to make them more accessible, relevant, and better known among career guidance advisors. This is the aim of the most recent initiative to develop a new Competency Profile for Career Development Professionals and to develop a pan-Canadian certification model. Building on consultations across Canada, the new Code of Ethics and Competency Profile for Career Development Professionals will underpin the establishment of a federal-level certification standard. It remains to be seen how they will be implemented across Canada.
>
> Source: Bezanson, Hopkins and Neault (2016[36]), "Career guidance and counselling in Canada: Still changing after all these years", *Canadian Journal of Counselling and Psychotherapy*, 50(3), https://cjc-rcc.ucalgary.ca/article/view/61123/pdf; Canadian Career Development Foundation and Canadian Council for Career Development (2021[33]), *The Canadian Standards & Guidelines for Career Development Practitioners (S&Gs)*, https://career-dev-guidelines.org/ (accessed 18 October 2021); http://ccdp-pcdc.ca (accessed 20 October 2021); OECD 2021 Policy Questionnaire 'Career guidance for adults in Canada'.

3.4.2. Voluntary provincial certifications are competency-based and follow a recognition of prior learning process

Five provinces have voluntary certifications for career guidance advisors available: Alberta, British Columbia, New Brunswick, Nova Scotia, and Ontario. The certifying bodies are the professional associations of career guidance advisors in the respective province. The criteria for certification and re-certification vary slightly from province to province but are grounded consistently in the Canadian Standards and Guidelines for Career Development Practitioners (Box 3.9). There is a mobility agreement and harmonised practices across these five bodies, so that Certified Career Development Practitioners (CCDPs) can move to another province without having to re-certify. In some provinces where certification is not yet available, including Saskatchewan and Manitoba, the professional associations have agreements for their practitioners to be certified in another province. Table 3.2 provides an overview of the existing certifications of career development practitioners in the different provinces.

The certification process in all five provinces is competency-based and follows a recognition of prior learning model. In practice, this means that a mix of relevant formal education and prior experience in the field is required. For practitioners with a Master's degree in an area related to career development, usually around one year of work experience is required in a career development role. For practitioners with very short or no formal education in a relevant field, a longer period of work experience in career development is required (up to 5 years of experience). Relevant formal education could be degrees and coursework in psychology, sociology, education, adult education and training, human resource management, labour economics, immigrant settlement, counselling or social work. While the precise requirements differ, voluntary certifications follow a similar approach across all five provinces.

As part of the recognition of prior learning approach to receive a professional certification, individuals must show documentation of previous work experience and education in career development. Often, career development associations ask applicants for a C.V. and job description from the current employer, as well as professional references. Applicants also have to demonstrate that they fulfil the competences outlined in the federal-level Competency Profile and show that they completed courses on ethics and professional conduct (usually 10 hours or coursework) as well as career development theories (usually 20 hours of coursework). In some cases, an evaluative assignment is required.

As certifications are organised and granted by provincial professional associations of career guidance, continuing membership with the respective association is also generally required. This includes a yearly membership fee and comes with opportunities for professional exchange and development. Generally, Certified Career Development Practitioners (CCDPs) need to renew their certification every 3 years. Professional associations of career guidance demand a minimum of 30 to 100 hours of continuing professional development, usually every 3 years, in order to keep the certification status.

Table 3.2. Certifications for career development practitioners across Canada

Province or territory	Assessment	Re-certification and mandatory professional development	Membership, Certification and Re-certification fees	Certifying body
Alberta (including the Northwest Territories)	Based on application and completion of 2 courses in career development (40h)	Every 3 years, minimum 60 hours of professional development per three year period	CAD 138 Yearly membership CAD 150 Certification fee CAD 100 Re-certification	https://www.careerdevelopment.ab.ca
British Columbia (including Yukon)	Based on application and completion of 2 courses in career development (30h)	No re-certification necessary, minimum of 25 hours of professional development every year	CAD 130 Yearly membership CAD 158 Certification fee	https://www.bccda.org
New Brunswick	Based on application and evaluation of 4 completed courses in career development (80h)	Every 3 years, minimum 30 hours of professional development per three year period	CAD 50 Yearly membership CAD 150 Certification fee CAD 75 Re-certification	http://www.nbcdag-gadcnb.ca
Nova Scotia	Based on application, work experience assessment, structured interview, and multiple-choice exam	Every 3 years, minimum of 60 hours of professional development per three year period	CAD 150 Yearly membership CAD 500 Certification fee CAD 250 Re-certification	https://nscda.ca/
Ontario	Based on application and completion of 2 courses in career development (30h)	Every 3 years, minimum of 60 hours professional development per three year period	CAD 50 Yearly membership CAD 225 Certification fee	https://cdpcbo.org

Source: OECD Policy questionnaire 'Career guidance for adults in Canada' and information by the Canadian Career Development Foundation (CCDF).

The certification is not a legal requirement to work in the profession in any province. Nevertheless, governments or employers may ask their staff or those of their third-party service providers to acquire the certification or prefer to hire certified practitioners for particular roles. This is the case in public employment services in Nova Scotia, for instance, where the government mandates the certification for certain positions in the Nova Scotia Works Centers through their funding program policies for employment assistance services. The Alberta government does not require its career guidance staff to be certified to work within the public employment service, but some employers prefer to hire Certified Career Development Practitioners. Albertan service providers are generally encouraged to have staff with specialised career guidance experience and training. In Quebec, where the system is a bit different as described in Box 3.8, some career guidance roles in the PES are restricted to advisors who have the C.O. license.

3.4.3. Occupational regulation of the career guidance field is uncommon in the OECD, but continuing training for practitioners can help improve service consistency

OECD countries generally do not regulate career guidance advisors as a distinct occupational group (OECD, 2021[28]). Although not determined in legislation, countries often define minimum training and qualifications for career guidance advisors in specific programmes. Generally, a relevant tertiary degree is required for adult career guidance advisors. Furthermore, advocacy by professional associations towards more regulation and professionalisation of the practice is an ongoing process in many countries (Gough and Neary, 2021[37]). Professionalisation could involve mandatory certifications (a license) or establishing voluntary certifications. Both could serve to give greater status to the profession, though evidence on the impact on quality is ambiguous (Box 3.10).

Increasingly across the OECD, specialised degrees on career guidance are available. In Germany, for example, dedicated bachelor's and master's degrees are offered by the German Federal Employment Agency through the University of Applied Labour Sciences (Bundesagentur für Arbeit, 2021[38]). Most employed career guidance specialists with the German Federal Employment Agency have obtained this qualification. Similarly, different educational institutions in Australia offer specialised degrees or certificates for career guidance, such as a certificate, graduate diploma or masters in career development (Career Development Association of Australia, 2021[39]). Other countries that have developed specialised academic degrees in career guidance include the Netherlands, Finland, Poland, Iceland, the UK, Switzerland or the United States (Cedefop, 2009[40]). In Canada, a career guidance degree does not currently exist outside Quebec. Creating one could enrich the landscape of training opportunities for career guidance advisors.

As in Canada, some OECD countries have competence frameworks in combination with voluntary certifications in place, as a way to make service provision more consistent. The rationale for regulating the practice of career guidance in this way is that the skills and qualifications of career guidance advisors are key for the success of adults in employment and learning. An example is the European Career Guidance Certificate (ECGC). Career guidance advisors in the United Kingdom can be registered by the United Kingdom Career Development Institute (CDI). Applicants have to show that they have a minimum qualification in career guidance, adhere to the CDI's Code of Ethics and undertake a minimum of 25 hours of professional development every year.

Box 3.10. Evidence on the effects of occupational regulation

Evidence from other occupations across OECD countries indicates that occupational regulations (voluntary certifications or mandatory licenses) have an ambiguous impact. More stringent occupational regulation of a professional group has shown to have an upward effect on wages within the profession. They also tend to increase prices for customers or clients and can lead to lower employment, productivity and labour mobility in the respective occupations (Bambalaite, Nicoletti and von Rueden, 2020[41]; Hermansen, 2019[42]; Koumenta and Pagliero, 2017[43]).

There is little empirical evidence demonstrating a positive link between the stringency of occupational regulations and the quality of services (Carroll and Gaston, 1981[44]; Kleiner and Kudrle, 2000[45]; Powell and Vorotnikov, 2011[46]; Kleiner, 2017[47]; Koumenta, Pagliero and Rostam-Afschar, 2019[48]). A historical analysis from the United States found that the introduction of licenses for midwives between 1900 and 1940 reduced maternal mortality by 6 to 7 percent, suggesting improvements in the quality of care (Anderson et al., 2016[49]). A study commissioned by the European Commission, however, suggests the opposite: the relaxation of entry requirements to legal occupations in Poland, for instance, showed little effect on the overall quality of legal services as measured through client surveys, while it led to an increase in the number of practicing lawyers. At the same time, an increase in educational requirements for driving instructors in the UK was linked to higher prices for driving lessons, worse student performance in driving tests and a decrease in the availability of the service (Koumenta, Pagliero and Rostam-Afschar, 2019[48]).

Recent OECD work (2020[50]) recommends considering whether occupational entry regulations are applied in a way that is proportional to the end they are supposed to achieve. The findings suggest that the focus of regulatory approaches should be shifted from the quality of inputs to the quality of outcomes. In the realm of career guidance, this means that instead of prioritising mandatory qualification requirements for practitioners, the focus should be on whether the outcomes of services have the desired quality and are in line with long-term policy goals. Another key area of policy action recommended by the OECD (2020[50]) is to extend mutual recognition of occupational regulations across jurisdictions. Recognition of career guidance certifications across provinces and territories could prevent artificial mobility restrictions for practitioners. The creation of a federal-level certification standard in Canada is an important step in this direction.

Independent of the certification for practitioners, continuing professional development is available in most province for those providing career guidance. Training programmes are generally in line with the federal-level Competency Profile (Box 3.9). Provincial professional associations of career guidance and professional organisations operating at a federal level, such as CCDF, CERIC or Career Professionals Canada (CPC), form an active network of associations, hosting numerous conferences, webinars and trainings. Most opportunities for continuing professional development are open to members and non-members alike, including external service providers or Indigenous practitioners. In New Brunswick, the participation in training courses is mandatory for government staff in some career guidance roles, and all approved training courses for certification are based on the federal-level Competency Profile. In Prince Edward Island, the provincial career guidance association receives government funding to provide workplace training for external service providers.

Standardising continuing professional development and making it more available is one way to professionalise and improve the practice of career guidance in Canada. Continuing education and training enables practitioners to keep up to date with developments in the field. For those who hold a provincial certification, some degree of continuing professional development is mandatory. But more could be done to make career guidance training available for a broader group of career and employment service providers. Many career and employment service providers in the OECD offer regular training opportunities to professionalise their staff. The Employment Service of Slovenia offers an annual catalogue of internal professional courses and trainings (in person or e-learning) and there is budget available to refer counsellors to external professional courses, trainings, conferences, study visits, and seminars. In Estonia, Eesti Töötukassa (the Estonian Unemployment Insurance Fund) organises training sessions and provides guidelines and information materials for advisors, and pays for the education of their employees who want to pursue a professional qualification as career counsellors (OECD, 2021[28]).

Provincial and territorial governments could strengthen and systematise continuing education and training for advisors who provide career guidance, in particular for those working in publicly-funded services. Ideally, they do so in co-operation with professional associations and organisations in the field of career guidance, and building on the Competency Profile for Career Development Professionals (Box 3.9). The updated federal-level Competency Profile can be used to benchmark advisor's skills to a common standard, and identify training needs in specific areas. An important aspect of continuing training is the use and interpretation of labour market information (see Section 3.2), which is also among the key skills outlined by the Competency Profile. A voluntary, pan-Canadian certification for career guidance can set a common competence standard and improve labour mobility for practitioners

The Canadian government has funded the first part of an initiative to develop a voluntary pan-Canadian certification for career development practitioners (CDPs) that would be available across all provinces and territories. This certification is based on the updated national Competence Framework for Career Development Professionals. The Canadian Career Development Foundation (CCDF) is leading the initiative, in tandem with several federal-level committees. The first project phase aimed at defining the career guidance profession, updating the existing competence framework for career development practitioners (the S&Gs) and developing a pan-Canadian professional certification programme (Canadian Career Development Foundation and Canadian Council for Career Development, 2021[33]). In doing so, the initiative relied on wide stakeholder engagement across the country with more than 1000 participants, in particular aiming at involving groups that were not part of previous S&G consultations. A policy questionnaire completed by members of the Canadian National Certification Committee sheds light on possible benefits and limitations of a pan-Canadian certification for career development practitioners (Box 3.11).

The second phase of the project focuses on implementation. Currently, a pan-Canadian certification programme is under development, in parallel to the development of a certifying body at the federal level. Together, these developments could provide the necessary infrastructure to support sustainable implementation of a pan-Canadian certification. Continuity in funding would also be essential.

Box 3.11. Benefits and limitations of a pan-Canadian certification for career development practitioners

Responses to the OECD 2021 Policy Questionnaire 'Certification for career development practitioners in Canada' provide insights into the perceived benefits and limitations of a pan-Canadian certification.

Most stakeholders are convinced that it would strengthen the profession by creating a consistent, recognisable standard for the competences of career development practitioners (CDPs). For CDPs, a pan-Canadian certification could align professional competences across provinces and territories, strengthen their professional identity, and improve job mobility across Canada. The professional community as a whole expects to see more public recognition and higher trust in career guidance, and a simplified, central system to regulate the practice, for instance, to resolve grievances. A federal-level certification might particularly benefit smaller provinces or territories which currently do not have the resources to implement their own certification programme. For clients or users of career guidance, a pan-Canadian certification programme promises higher consistency and quality of services.

There are also perceived limitations of a pan-Canadian certification for career development practitioners. First, experts were concerned there may not be sufficient resources to fully implement and administer the programme. Also, there might be limited interest and funding by employers or provider organisations to adopt certification as a requirement for their staff, as it could increase costs for services. Although not mentioned in the questionnaire responses, establishing the certification as a requirement might also create entry barriers, potentially limiting the supply of practitioners in the field. Generally, occupational regulation is a provincial responsibility, which means that the adherence to a pan-Canadian certification needs to remain on a voluntary basis.

Consistent with previous OECD research (2020[50]), the stringency and scope of application of a pan-Canadian certification should be proportional to the end of achieving high-quality, inclusive services for adults in Canada. Establishing a pan-Canadian certification that remains voluntary might provide a foundation to improve consistency in service delivery, while avoiding undue barriers to entry and loss of flexibility.

Note: The Policy Questionnaire was sent to all members of the National Certification Steering Committee.
Source: OECD 2021 Policy Questionnaire 'Certification for career development practitioners in Canada.'

Assessment and recommendations

Monitoring outcomes supports oversight of service quality by provincial and territorial governments, and could be done in a more systematic way. Monitoring outcomes also helps private providers to document and track their performance. Evidence-based digital tools such as PRIME are promising to help improve outcome monitoring. Outcome-based contract management with third-party providers has many advantages, although its particular design and implementation matters for incentivising sustainable, high-quality service provision.

At present, there is not a strong enough link between the outcomes that providers monitor and more long-term policy objectives within provinces and territories. Career guidance policy goals can be part of an overarching framework for employment or skills development of adults. A good example is the framework that is being developed for Nova Scotia Works, where career guidance is part of a larger employment strategy.

- Provinces and territories should systematically monitor the outcomes of publicly-funded career guidance services in line with long-term policy objectives.

Continuous learning matters for those who provide career guidance as much as it matters for their clients. Continuing professional development for career guidance advisors allows them to stay informed about recent labour market developments, as well as about recent developments in the field. While continuing professional development is a requirement for those who are certified or licensed (in the case of Quebec), more could be done to offer training for advisors who work in publicly-funded services. In order to reinforce a common standard of service provision, training should be underpinned by the federal-level Competence Profile for career development.

- Provinces and territories should strengthen training for advisors providing career guidance in publicly-funded services, especially on the use of labour market information.

Requirements for the training and qualifications of career guidance advisors vary across Canada, which contributes to inconsistency in service delivery across and within provinces and territories. At the same time, Canada is a front-runner in many ways: in creating the first competence framework for practitioners; establishing a federal-level certification initiative; and maintaining an active professional community through career guidance associations and other stakeholder organisations. While making certifications a requirement to work in the career guidance field could have unintended negative effects and create entry barriers, a voluntary, pan-Canadian certification can remove mobility barriers for practitioners and help to establish a common standard of practice.

- Federal, provincial and territorial governments should in co-ordination support and fund the implementation of a voluntary, pan-Canadian certification for career development practitioners.

References

Anderson, D. et al. (2016), "The Effect of Occupational Licensing on Consumer Welfare: Early Midwifery Laws and Maternal Mortality", *JEL No I18,J08*, No. No. 22456, NBER Working Paper, http://www.nber.org/papers/w22456 (accessed on 2 November 2021). [49]

Bambalaite, I., G. Nicoletti and C. von Rueden (2020), "Occupational entry regulations and their effects on productivity in services: Firm-level evidence", *OECD Economics Department Working Papers*, No. 1605, OECD Publishing, Paris, https://dx.doi.org/10.1787/c8b88d8b-en. [41]

Barnes, S. et al. (2020), *Lifelong guidance policy and practice in the EU: trends, challenges and opportunities*, European Commission, http://dx.doi.org/10.2767/91185. [2]

Bezanson, L., S. Hopkins and R. Neault (2016), "Career Guidance and Counselling in Canada: Still Changing After All These Years", *Canadian Journal of Counselling and Psychotherapy*, Vol. 50/3, pp. 219-239, https://cjc-rcc.ucalgary.ca/article/view/61123/pdf. [36]

Bimrose, J. and S. Barnes (2008), *Adult career progression & advancement: a five year study of the effectiveness of guidance*, Department for Education and Skills; Warwick Institute for Employment Research, https://warwick.ac.uk/fac/soc/ier/publications/2008/eg_report_4_years_on_final.pdf (accessed on 29 January 2021). [3]

Bundesagentur für Arbeit (2021), *BA-Studium: Dualer Studiengang „Beratung für Bildung, Beruf und Beschäftigung"*, https://www.arbeitsagentur.de/ba-karriere/studium-beratung (accessed on 28 September 2021). [38]

Canadian Career Development Foundation and Canadian Council for Career Development (2021), *The Canadian Standards & Guidelines for Career Development Practitioners, CDP Competence*, https://career-dev-guidelines.org/cdp-competence/ (accessed on 21 October 2021). [33]

Career Development Association of Australia (2021), *Study Career Development*, https://www.cdaa.org.au/about-career-development/study-career-development (accessed on 28 September 2021). [39]

Carroll, S. and R. Gaston (1981), "Occupational Restrictions and the Quality of Service Received: Some Evidence", *Southern Economic Journal*, Vol. 47/4, pp. 959-976, https://doi.org/10.2307/1058155. [44]

Cedefop (2009), "Professionalising career guidance: Practitioner competences and qualification routes in Europe", https://www.cedefop.europa.eu/files/5193_en.pdf (accessed on 21 January 2022). [40]

CERIC (2019), *2019 Survey of Career Service Professionals*, https://ceric.ca/2019-survey-of-career-service-professionals/ (accessed on 19 October 2021). [32]

Department of Education Skills and Employment (2021), *New Employment Service Trial (NEST) Guidelines*, https://www.dese.gov.au/collections/new-employment-service-trial-nest-guidelines (accessed on 23 January 2022). [27]

Employment Nova Scotia (2021), *Nova Scotia Employment Assistance Services Policy*. [30]

Employment Nova Scotia (2019), *Nova Scotia Works Accountability Framework Strategic Plan*. [29]

ESDC (2021), *Skills for Success – Assessment and training tools*, [15]
https://www.canada.ca/en/services/jobs/training/initiatives/skills-success/tools.html?category=Individual&type=Training (accessed on 29 October 2021).

European Commission (2015), *An in-depth analysis of adult learning policies and their* [7]
effectiveness in Europe, Publications Office of the European Union, Luxembourg,
https://op.europa.eu/en/publication-detail/-/publication/c8c38dc9-89d0-11e5-b8b7-01aa75ed71a1/language-en (accessed on 28 September 2021).

Fortson, K. et al. (2017), *Providing Public Workforce Services to Job Seekers: 30-Month Impact* [14]
Findings on the WIA Adult and Dislocated Worker Programs, Mathematica Policy Research,
Washington, DC, https://www.mathematica.org/publications/providing-public-workforce-services-to-job-seekers-30-month-impact-findings-on-the-wia-adult (accessed on
5 November 2021).

Gough, J. and S. Neary (2021), "The Career Development Profession: Professionalisation, [37]
Professionalism, and Professional Identity", *The Oxford Handbook of Career Development*,
pp. 256-268, http://dx.doi.org/10.1093/OXFORDHB/9780190069704.013.19.

Government of Alberta (2021), *Income and Employment Supports Policy Manual -* [26]
Accountability, http://www.humanservices.alberta.ca/AWOnline/3813.html (accessed on
16 September 2021).

Government of Canada (2021), *Evaluation of the Job Match Service connecting Job Seekers to* [22]
Canadian Employers. Final Report, https://www.canada.ca/content/dam/esdc-edsc/documents/corporate/reports/evaluations/job-match-connecting-job-seekers-employers/jobMatchReport-en.pdf (accessed on 6 October 2021).

Government of Canada (2021), *Job Bank*, https://www.jobbank.gc.ca/home (accessed on [23]
30 June 2021).

Government of Ontario (2003), *Policy/Program Memorandum 132*, [16]
https://www.ontario.ca/document/education-ontario-policy-and-program-direction/policyprogram-memorandum-132 (accessed on 29 October 2021).

Graversen, B. and J. van Ours (2008), "How to help unemployed find jobs quickly: Experimental [13]
evidence from a mandatory activation program", *Journal of Public Economics*, Vol. 92/10-11,
pp. 2020-2035, http://dx.doi.org/10.1016/J.JPUBECO.2008.04.013.

Hermansen, M. (2019), "Occupational licensing and job mobility in the United States", *OECD* [42]
Economics Department Working Papers, No. 1585, OECD Publishing, Paris,
https://dx.doi.org/10.1787/4cc19056-en.

Hughes, D. et al. (2002), *The Economic Benefits of Guidance*, Centre for Guidance Studies, [6]
https://www.researchgate.net/profile/Sara-Bosley/publication/238078155_The_Economic_Benefits_of_Guidance_The_Economic_The_Economic_Benefits_of_Benefits_of_Guidance_Guidance/links/54e631a00cf2bff5a4f45f53/The-Economic-Benefits-of-Guidance-The-Economic-The-Economic-Benefits-of-Benefits-of-Guidance-Guidance.pdf (accessed on 27 September 2021).

Kidd, J., C. Jackson and W. Hirsh (2003), "The outcomes of effective career discussion at work", *Journal of Vocational Behavior*, Vol. 62/1, pp. 119-133, http://dx.doi.org/10.1016/S0001-8791(02)00027-1. [5]

Killeen, J. and J. Kidd (1991), *Learning outcomes of guidance: a review of recent research*, Department of Employment; National Institute of Careers Education and Counselling. [11]

Kleiner, M. (2017), "The influence of occupational licensing and regulation", *IZA World of Labour*, Vol. 392, http://dx.doi.org/10.15185/izawol.392. [47]

Kleiner, M. and R. Kudrle (2000), "Does Regulation Affect Economic Outcomes? The Case of Dentistry", *Journal of Law & Economics*, Vol. 43/2, pp. 547-582, https://doi.org/10.1086/467465. [45]

Koumenta, M. and M. Pagliero (2017), *Measuring Prevalence and Labour Market Impacts of Occupational Regulation in the EU*, European Commission; Publications Office of the European Union, https://www.google.com/url?sa=t&rct=j&q=&esrc=s&source=web&cd=&cad=rja&uact=8&ved=2ahUKEwjeyPf0ns_1AhUO4YUKHekiA5sQFnoECAMQAQ&url=https%3A%2F%2Fec.europa.eu%2Fdocsroom%2Fdocuments%2F20362%2Fattachments%2F1%2Ftranslations%2Fen%2Frenditions%2Fnative&usg=AOv (accessed on 12 December 2021). [43]

Koumenta, M., M. Pagliero and D. Rostam-Afschar (2019), *Effects of Regulation on Service Quality*, European Commission; Publications Office of the European Union, https://data.europa.eu/doi/10.2873/910094. [48]

Lane, M. et al. (2017), *An economic evaluation of the National Careers Service*, Department of Education (United Kingdom), https://assets.publishing.service.gov.uk/government/uploads/system/uploads/attachment_data/file/603929/National_Careers_Service_economic_evaluation.pdf. [9]

Langenbucher, K. and M. Vodopivec (2022), "Paying for results: Contracting out employment services through outcome-based payment schemes in OECD countries", *OECD Social, Employment and Migration Working Papers*, No. 267, OECD Publishing, Paris, https://dx.doi.org/10.1787/c6392a59-en. [25]

Liu, S., J. Huang and M. Wang (2014), "Effectiveness of Job Search Interventions: A Meta-Analytic Review", *Psychological Bulletin*, Vol. 140/4, pp. 1009-1041, http://dx.doi.org/10.1037/a0035923. [12]

LMIC (2021), *About*, https://lmic-cimt.ca/about/ (accessed on 27 October 2021). [18]

LMIC (2021), "LMI User Guide Workshop with Career Development Practitioners. Final Summary". [20]

LMIC (2019), *From Data to Information: What LMI do career development practitioners need?*, LMI Insights Report no. 20, https://lmic-cimt.ca/publications-all/lmi-insights-report-no-20-from-data-to-information-what-lmi-do-career-development-practitioners-need/ (accessed on 3 November 2021). [21]

LMIC (2018), *Strategic Plan 2018 - 2020*, https://lmic-cimt.ca/wp-content/uploads/2020/01/strategic-plan.pdf (accessed on 3 November 2021). [19]

Maguire, M. (2004), "Measuring the Outcomes of Career Guidance", *International Journal for Educational and Vocational Guidance*, Vol. 4, pp. 179-192, https://link.springer.com/content/pdf/10.1007/s10775-005-1022-1.pdf (accessed on 24 September 2021). [4]

OCCOQ (2021), *Ordre des conseillers et conseillères d'orientation du Québec*, https://www.orientation.qc.ca/ (accessed on 5 August 2021). [34]

OCCOQ (2021), *Rapport Annuel 2020/2021*, https://www.orientation.qc.ca/medias/iw/Rapport-annuel-OCCOQ-2020-2021.pdf (accessed on 23 September 2021). [35]

OECD (2021), *Career Guidance for Adults in a Changing World of Work*, Getting Skills Right, OECD Publishing, Paris, https://dx.doi.org/10.1787/9a94bfad-en. [28]

OECD (2020), *Workforce Innovation to Foster Positive Learning Environments in Canada*, Getting Skills Right, OECD Publishing, Paris, https://dx.doi.org/10.1787/a92cf94d-en. [31]

OECD (2016), *Assessing and Anticipating Changing Skill Needs*, OECD Publishing, Paris, http://dx.doi.org/10.1787/9789264252073-en. [17]

Percy, C. and V. Dodd (2021), "The Economic Outcomes of Career Development Programmes", in Robertson, P., T. Hooley and P. McCash (eds.), *The Oxford Handbook of Career Development*, Oxford University Press, http://dx.doi.org/10.1093/OXFORDHB/9780190069704.013.4. [1]

Powell, B. and E. Vorotnikov (2011), "Real Estate Continuing Education: Rent Seeking or Improvement in Service Quality?", *Eastern Economic Journal*, Vol. 38/1, pp. 57-73, http://dx.doi.org/10.1057/EEJ.2010.51. [46]

Reavley, M. (2013), "The Impact of Providing Labour Market Information Training on Trainees' Perceptions of Job related Self-Efficacy: A Comparison of the Influence of Two Delivery Methods on Expressions of Competence and Confidence", *The Canadian Journal of Career Development.*, Vol. 12/2. [8]

Tyers, C. and A. Sinclair (2005), *Intermediate Impacts of Advice and Guidance. Research Report No 638*, Institute for Employment Studies, https://webarchive.nationalarchives.gov.uk/ukgwa/20130401151715/http://www.education.gov.uk/publications/eOrderingDownload/RR638.pdf (accessed on 24 September 2021). [10]

Verhagen, A. (2021), "Opportunities and drawbacks of using artificial intelligence for training", *OECD Social, Employment and Migration Working Papers*, No. 266, OECD Publishing, Paris, https://dx.doi.org/10.1787/22729bd6-en. [24]

von Rueden, C. and I. Bambalaite (2020), "Measuring occupational entry regulations: A new OECD approach", *OECD Economics Department Working Papers*, No. 1606, OECD Publishing, Paris, https://dx.doi.org/10.1787/296dae6b-en. [50]

Note

[1] Among the survey respondents who received career guidance services and were satisfied or very satisfied with them, 1 469 were living in urban, and 135 in rural areas. Similarly, 1 436 respondents in this group were classified as "prime age" (age 25-54), and 169 as "older" (above age 54). Further details about sample sizes and methodology can be found at the end of the report in Annex B.

Annex A. Responses to policy questionnaires

This report relies upon information collected by the OECD Policy Questionnaire 'Career Guidance for Adults in Canada', which focused on how career guidance is organised, funded, and provided. It was completed by Employment and Social Development Canada (ESDC) in June 2020. It was later distributed to provinces and territories through the Forum of Labour Market Ministers and the Council of Ministers of Education in Canada. Responses were provided by provincial employment and labour officials and/or provincial education officials in July and August 2021, as summarised in the table below.

Table A A.1. Provinces and territories that responded to the OECD 2021 Policy Questionnaire 'Career Guidance for Adults in Canada'

Province or Territory	Ministry of Employment and Labour	Ministry of Education	Not answered
Alberta	X	X	
British Columbia		X	
Manitoba			X
New Brunswick	X		
Newfoundland and Labrador			X
Northwest Territories			X
Nova Scotia	X		
Nunavut			X
Ontario	X	X	
Prince Edward Island			X
Quebec	X		
Saskatchewan	X		
Yukon			X

Note: In the provinces where both the Ministry of Labour and the Ministry of Education is marked, the two ministries collaborated to submit a common response to the policy questionnaire. In some provinces and territories, the Ministry of Employment and Labour is also responsible for post-secondary education or adult learning, including in New Brunswick and Nunavut.

A separate policy questionnaire, the OECD 2021 Policy Questionnaire 'Certification for career development practitioners in Canada' focused on the voluntary, pan-Canadian certification for career guidance advisors. It was sent to all members of the National Certification Steering Committee in July 2021 and informed the analysis of the benefits and limitations of a pan-Canadian certification standard.

Annex B. Methodology note on the Survey of Career Guidance for Adults

This report uses data collected in the OECD 2020/2021 Survey of Career Guidance for Adults (SCGA). The SCGA was conducted to better understand adults' experience with career guidance services and to improve international data on its use, coverage and inclusiveness. For Canada, the data collection and methodology differed from that of other countries that participated in the survey in certain respects.

First two phases of SCGA data collection

Data collection for the SCGA was carried out in two initial phases. The first phase of data collection took place between mid-June and early-July 2020 in six countries: Chile, France, Germany, Italy, New Zealand and the United States. The second phase of data collection took place in November 2020 in Argentina, Brazil and Mexico. Fieldwork was conducted by Cint[1] and the sample was restricted to adults aged 25-64, to target those who had left initial education.

The survey was prepared in five languages (English, French, German, Italian and Spanish) and disseminated via an online survey to a panel of registered individuals. A stratified sample methodology imposed quotas to have a representative sample of each country's population in terms of age, gender and region. The age and gender quotas were based on UN World Population Prospects statistics,[2] while the regional quotas were based on Cint's data. Education quotas were added in the second phase of data collection (for more details, see OECD (2021[1])).

After data collection, two quality checks were applied. First, if a respondent completed the survey in two minutes or less, the respondent was excluded. This is based on the assumption that the survey takes more than two minutes to complete with appropriate consideration. Second, if a respondent did not answer the final question of the survey, they were also excluded. This was to ensure that only respondents who completed the full survey were captured in the final dataset.

Data collection for the Canadian survey

The data collection and methodology for Canada differed from those of the other countries in several respects.

First, for the Canadian survey, some questions and answer options were phrased differently, and additional questions and answer options were added. This was done at the request of the Canadian partners in order to tailor the survey better to the Canadian context. For instance, the Canadian survey asked adults, "In the past 5 years, have you used a *career service?*"[3] In the other countries in the survey, adults were asked instead, "In the past 5 years, have you *spoken to a career guidance advisor?*" These differences in question wording likely had an impact on the cross-country comparability of the data on the use of career guidance.

Also, the Canadian survey was carried out by a different survey provider, who applied a slightly different methodology than the one used by Cint. Data sampling was carried out by Ipsos Limited Partnership and the data collection process was overseen by the Canadian Labour Market Information Council (LMIC).

Data were collected online between 24 February 2021 and 25 March 2021 through both English and French surveys. As with the other countries, the sample was stratified by provinces[4], age, gender and education using the latest Census data (2016). The sample was restricted to adults aged 25-64.

Ipsos used a two-step implementation method to collect data for the Canadian survey. First, the initial survey design targeted a sample of career service users (2 000 respondents) separately from a sample of non-users (1 000 respondents). Then, to be able to compare the two groups, weights were introduced in the sample and were estimated from a representative online omnibus survey designed to measure the incidence of career guidance use among the general population of adult Canadians (18+). Out of 2 001 total observations in the omnibus survey, 405 individuals reported having used a career service, for an estimated incidence rate of 20%.

The above-mentioned quality checks were not carried out for the Canadian survey.

Cross-country comparison

To improve cross-country comparison, this report features weighted data. The weighting served to mitigate differences related to the fact that education quotas were not included in the first phase of data collection but were included for both the second phase and for Canada. For those countries from the first phase of data collection, for which education quotas were not imposed, education weights were constructed using OECD data (2020[2]).

Figure A B.1 compares the composition of the country-level samples with the composition of the actual population in each country in terms of gender, age and education. Thanks to quotas, the sample shares are very close to those of the actual population on gender in all countries. The sample is younger than the actual population in all countries, owing to the fact that older adults are less likely to complete online surveys than younger adults. The sample is over-educated relative to the actual population in some countries (Argentina, Brazil, Chile, and Mexico) and under-educated relative to the actual population in other countries (Canada, France, Germany, Italy, New Zealand and the United States).

Figure A B.1. Sample composition by age, gender and education group, compared to the composition of the actual population, weighted data

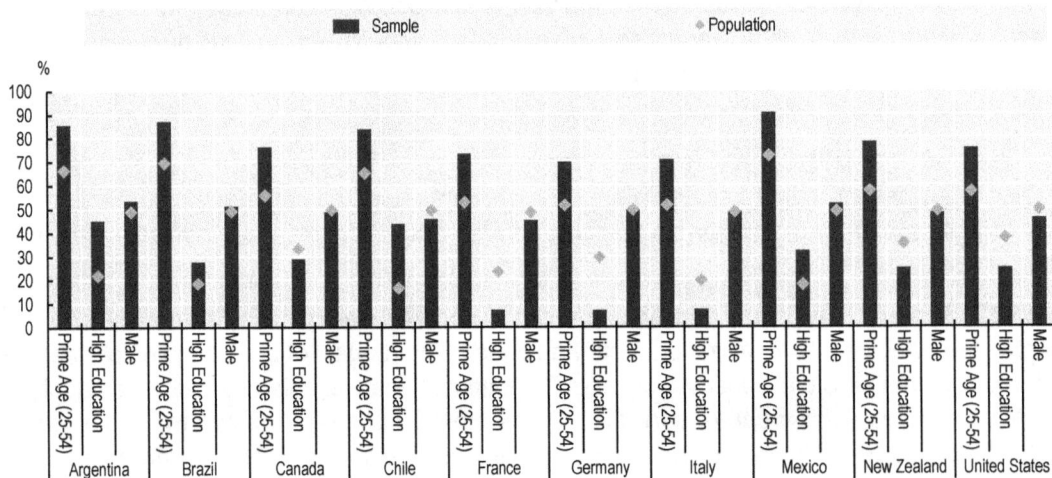

Note: The denominator is adults aged 25 to 64.
Source: The sample composition by age, gender and education is drawn from the OECD 2020/2021 Survey of Career Guidance for Adults (SCGA). The population distribution of age and gender were extracted from the UN 2019 Revision of World Population Prospects (https://population.un.org/wpp/). For population estimates by education group, OECD (2020[2]), *OECD Education at a Glance 2020: OECD Indicators*, https://dx.doi.org/10.1787/69096873-en, was used.

Another factor that affects cross-country comparability of the data is timing. In particular, the online survey was conducted at different stages of the COVID-19 crisis over 2020 and 2021. This might have implications on the response rates and composition of respondents, given that the time a person would have to complete an online survey may have changed in the context of confinement, teleworking or layoffs. The use of quotas mitigates this effect. The differences in the timing of the survey may also have implications on the reported use of career services due to measures adopted to tackle the employment effects of the pandemic. Table A B.1 shows the final sample sizes for each country in the SCGA.

Table A B.1. Final sample size by country

Country	Sample Size
Argentina	1 023
Brazil	982
Canada	3 564
Chile	963
France	988
Germany	979
Italy	1 022
Mexico	1 014
New Zealand	926
United States	970

Source: OECD 2020/2021 Survey of Career Guidance for Adults (SCGA).

References

OECD (2021), "Methodology note on the Survey of Career Guidance for Adults", in *Career Guidance for Adults in a Changing World of Work*, OECD Publishing, Paris, https://dx.doi.org/10.1787/6b6c6c86-en.   [1]

OECD (2020), *Education at a Glance 2020: OECD Indicators*, OECD Publishing, Paris, https://dx.doi.org/10.1787/69096873-en.   [2]

Notes

[1] Cint is a digital insights gathering platform (www.cint.com). The Cint platform and products comply with standards and certifications set out by various market research associations including ESOMAR, MRS, ARF, MRIA, AMA, AMSRO and Insights Association and ISO 20 252 quality standards.

[2] https://population.un.org/wpp/.

[3] The survey defined career services as follows: "Career services are offered across Canada through public employment services, community based agencies, educational institutions, workplaces and private providers. Career services offer a range of supports, including:

- Helping you to access information to help you make your career-related decisions (e.g., wage information, job prospects, cost of living, etc.)

- Helping you to understand your career options and choose your career direction

- Helping you to get the skills/credentials/training you need to pursue your career goals

- Helping you to get a job or start a business

- Helping you to keep your job or grow within your position/organisation

- Addressing personal/life issues that may be preventing you from moving forward with your goals"

[4] Alberta, British Columbia, Manitoba, New Brunswick, Newfoundland and Labrador, Nova Scotia, Ontario, Prince Edward Island, Quebec, and Saskatchewan. The territories were not part of the stratification because of extremely low sample sizes.

Annex C. Sensitivity analysis

In Canada, as elsewhere, the shares for urban areas are larger in the OECD 2020/2021 Survey of Career Guidance for Adults (SCGA) than in the actual population. The percentage of the sample living in urban areas was 87% in Canada, whereas only 82% of the actual Canadian population lives in urban areas. This is likely because people in rural areas tend to participate less in online surveys than those in urban areas, possibly due to lack of access to the internet or digital technologies. Table A C.1 shows results from a simple sensitivity analysis where the use of career guidance within urban and rural areas is held fixed, while the share of adults in each group is adjusted to match the population. A weighted average is computed, multiplying the share of adults in each group by their use of career guidance, then summing up across the two groups. The results of the sensitivity analysis show that, all other things being equal, if the regional composition in the sample matched the actual regional composition in the population, the share of adults who used career guidance in the last five years would be 20.0%, negligibly lower than in the sample (20.3%). It suggests that over-representation in urban areas does not have a large impact on the accuracy of the overall findings.

Table A C.1. Sensitivity analysis

	Share in the sample	Share in the population	Use of career guidance based on the sample
Urban	86.5%	81.6%	21.3%
Rural	13.5%	18.4%	14.1%
Total incidence rate (based on the sample)			20.3%
Total incidence rate (using population shares, hypothetical)			20.0%

Source: OECD 2020/2021 Survey of Career Guidance for Adults (SCGA). The population distribution was extracted from the UN 2019 Revision of World Population Prospects, (https://population.un.org/wpp/).

www.ingramcontent.com/pod-product-compliance
Lightning Source LLC
Chambersburg PA
CBHW082109210326
41599CB00033B/6641